Guide to Search and Rescue Dogs

Angela Eaton Snovak

With Full-color Photographs
Drawings by Michele Earle-Bridges

BARRON'S

SEARCH DOG

Acknowledgments

Genuine gratitude goes to the search dog handlers who have shared their expertise and time with me throughout the years. In particular, Fran Lieser, a co-founder of Search and Rescue Dogs of Colorado, shared her wealth of knowledge and experience in search and rescue and canine behavior. A special thanks also goes to Grietje Sloan and her search dog, Cello, for years spent together training and searching in every kind of weather imaginable throughout the seasons, day and night. We shrugged off the mountain lion tracks in the snow in order to keep working our dogs! Thanks also to Carol Knock and Tri Sorts Kennel for sweet Isis, my search dog and partner for over fourteen years, and for lively, creative Shakti, the puppy following in her paw prints at a very fast pace. My husband Mike has been an incredible partner and offers his expert advice on all the technical aspects of search and rescue and mountaineering. Finally, to all of the search dog handlers who still get excited at the thrill of watching their fabulous dogs solve incredible problems, thank you for your generosity, humility, and service.

All inquiries should be addressed to:
Barron's Educational Series, Inc.
250 Wireless Boulevard
Hauppauge, New York 11788
http://www.barronseduc.com

International Standard Book No. 0-7641-2418-8

Library of Congress Catalog Card No. 2003061725

Library of Congress Cataloging-in-Publication Data
Snovak, Angela Eaton.
   Guide to search and rescue dogs / by Angela Eaton Snovak.
     p. cm.
   Includes bibliographical references (p.) and index.
   ISBN 0-7641-2418-8 (alk. paper)
    1. Seach dogs. 2. Rescue dogs. I. Title: Guide to search and rescue dogs. II. Title: Search and rescue dogs. III. Title.

SF428.73.S66 2004
636.73—dc22   2003061725

Printed in China
9 8 7 6 5 4 3 2 1

About the the Author

Angela Eaton Snovak became interested in Search and Rescue (SAR) dogs while living in Europe. Observing avalanche dogs at work in the Alps fascinated her, but on her return to the United States, she could not locate any SAR dog trainers. She found such trainers after moving to Colorado, and became active in all phases of SAR work. Since 1983, she has trained dogs and handlers, lectured and written extensively on all phases of this ultimate expression of dogs' service to humankind.

Cover Photos

Front cover: Michael Snovak (top photo); Nance Photography (2nd and 3rd photos from top); Kent and Donna Dannen (bottom photo). Back cover: Nance Photography. Inside front cover: Michael Snovak. Inside back cover: Nance Photography.

Photo Credits

Michael Snovak: 2, 7, 9, 10, 11, 13, 16, 17, 20, 21, 24, 25, 27, 29, 31, 32, 37, 38, 40, 45, 48, 51, 54, 56, 60, 62, 64, 69, 71, 72, 73, 74, 77, 79, 81, 86, 88, 90, 93, 96, 97, 98, 101 (top and bottom), 104, 106, 108, 110, 112, 113, 114, 115, 121, 128, 130, 132, 136, 137, 138, 141, 143, 146, 147, 149, 151, 154, 157, 161, 162, 164, 165 (bottom), 176, 179, 180, 181, 182, 184; Nance Photography: 3, 18, 35, 43, 46, 49, 50, 58, 61, 68, 70, 111, 118, 131, 145, 165 top, 183; Kent and Donna Dannen: 8.

Important Note

This book is intended to introduce readers to the field of canine search and rescue. It is designed as an overview of the various aspects of search and rescue dogs and to help the reader understand the complexities of raising and training a dog toward certification in this field. The author and the publisher consider it important to point out that the advice given in this book is meant primarily for normally developed dogs of excellent physical health and good character. Not all dogs or people are suited for search and rescue work.

As stated throughout the book, it is the responsibility of each person to take reasonable precautions and to use good judgment when working with their dog under all circumstances. The situations described in the book are based on a level of expertise that is gained only through years of experience achieved through careful training and practice. The training lessons and techniques outlined in the book are intended as a guide for people interested in training a dog toward search and rescue or those who want to understand how search dogs are trained. Common to all training methods, the outcome depends on the capabilities of the individuals involved. There is no guarantee for success in the specialized and technical field of canine search and rescue.

Contents

Chapter One

What Is Canine Search and Rescue?

Search and rescue (SAR) is an aspect of emergency services in which federal, state, and local agencies coordinate, deploy, and manage trained, certified teams to look for, rescue, or recover lost and/or injured people. Search and rescue techniques are as old as humankind. Although we have no written record, there is no doubt that when children of cave dwellers became lost, their families and members of their tribe certainly worked together to search for and rescue them from danger and to return them to safety. Today, this type of search is referred to as *wilderness search and rescue* and is only one aspect of several search and rescue disciplines used in today's world. Of the various components of search and rescue, one of the most valuable and interesting is the use of dogs. We know that dogs have been credited with finding people and saving lives since humans and canines realized one another's value. In relatively recent times, people began to realize and take advantage of dogs' remarkable physiology to find and rescue lost and injured people.

One of the many aspects of search and rescue in which trained and certified dogs are used is the type of wilderness search just described, where dogs search for, locate, and rescue people who've become lost in remote areas. The missing people are returned to their loved ones, often after life-saving emergency medical procedures. Some other search and rescue specialties where dogs are a critical resource include finding and rescuing people buried by snow slides (avalanche rescue), locating drowned victims (water search), locating and rescuing people who are trapped after a natural or man-made calamity (urban or disaster search and rescue), and locating decomposing human bodies and/or trace evidence of human bodies above and below ground (cadaver search or human remains detection). Although each of these specialties requires its own set of resources and skills, quite often teams trained to respond to missions use a combination of techniques. Some basic skills are required from dogs in all types of situations. These include finding and following scent, agility, and obedience. The handlers are also required to have a set of basic skills in order to work effectively with their dogs. Any of these skills could be needed at any time, whether a team is searching for a lost child in the wilderness after dark, for a snowboarder after an avalanche, or for several hundred people in the wake of a disaster in the middle of a city.

The most obvious skill required of a search dog is the ability to deliberately identify and follow a specific scent. Two scenting techniques used in canine search and rescue are air scenting and trailing. Most search dogs are trained to either air scent or trail to locate victims, although some canine search teams require their dogs to use both techniques. Even a dog trained for a particular technique may use the other when certain conditions arise. Either way, at all times

An avalanche dog finds human scent that percolates to the surface through snow.

during a search, handlers must be able to determine whether their dog is following scent on the ground or in the air, because this knowledge may contribute to the vital information they need about the missing person's location.

Air scenting refers to the dog's ability to identify scent in the air as it's emanating directly from a person. A dog that is air scenting can be given a particular scent to identify, but may also identify the scent of any person in an area and does not require an article with an identifying scent. The use of air scenting techniques in wilderness search may also be referred to as *area search,* because it is applied in a pre-defined area.

When a dog follows residual scent that settles on the ground as a person walks through an area, it's referred to as *trailing*. A trailing dog requires an article with the scent of the particular person (or a *scent article*) it's expected to find, to determine which scent to follow. A trailing dog follows specific scent that has dropped from a particular individual wherever it settles, on all types of surfaces.

Trailing dogs are distinguished from *tracking dogs* in that tracking dogs follow bacteria growing on the ground and vegetation that has been disturbed as an individual walks. *Tracking* is a style familiar to many dog owners who compete in dog trials. Tracking, as defined here, is not appropriate for most search and rescue situations, because the ground is walked over by many other searchers who create more ground disturbance in the area, often before the search dog arrives on a mission.

Various situations require that both the dog and handler be physically adept. Therefore, agility is also a skill needed by a search dog team. Because most situations in search and rescue are physically demanding, the dog team must be able to deal with challenging and potentially dangerous obstacles. Some type of agility training is as important for the handler as it is for the dog. Formal agility training can enhance search training, but agility conditioning using real situations is extremely valuable, as well. This may include following the dog across streams, through rock outcroppings, into large piles of rubble or climbing up avalanche debris fields where the chunks of snow are as large as cars.

Another important basic skill is obedience. The handler needs to be able to rely on the dog to respond to commands at all times. Some basic responses a handler is required to teach a search dog are to *sit* or *lie down, stop* immediately, *wait* until further instruction, come without hesitation, and *stay* until the handler releases the dog. Most search dogs understand many additional commands, because they face a wide range of situations in which their handlers continually communicate directions and commands. The dog's handler is responsible for ensuring the safety of the dog, and failure of a dog to respond immediately and

A water search dog locates the scent of drowning victims as the scent rises to the surface through the water.

consistently to these commands may result in injury or even a life-threatening accident. Therefore, the handler is responsible for making sure the dog is completely obedient and reliable before embarking on any search mission.

Why Are Dogs Used in Search and Rescue?

Dogs and humans have worked in partnership for thousands of years. Hunting game and herding flocks together throughout the ages has created an enduring bond. Humans have realized that a dog's special abilities and skills can extend our own capabilities. A natural evolution of this partnership has been the use of dogs in search and rescue. In fact, search dogs have become much more widely used in an *official* capacity in search and rescue over the past few decades, and are considered an indispensable element of search and rescue around the world.

The ability to hunt prey by following its scent is inherent in a dog's nature. Many dog owners recognize their dog's ability at a very early age to find food or toys using its nose. According to studies described in the book, *Scent, Training to Track, Search and Rescue* by Milo D. Pearsall and Hugo Verbruggen, M.D., large dog breeds have approximately 150 to 220 million olfactory receptor cells, and can consistently detect extremely minute particles of scent under remarkably adverse conditions. In comparison, humans have approximately 5 million olfactory receptor cells. It has also been said that a dog remembers the scent of anyone with whom it's ever come into contact throughout its lifetime. Another excellent source for learning more about the anatomy and physiology of dogs as it pertains to their olfactory system is *Scent and the Scenting Dog* by William G. Syrotuck (Barkleigh Productions, Inc., 1972). This book is still considered to be required reading for search dog handlers.

Many search dogs are trained to discriminate between a specific scent and any other scent, ignoring the scent of other people. These dogs stay focused on the unique scent of the lost person throughout the search. When searching for a lost person, the dog's ability to discriminate enables it to find any trace of that individual, including anything the person has touched. This is done by asking the dog to sniff an article, or *scent article,* worn or handled by the missing person to identify the scent of the individual upon whom the search is focused. Although the dog

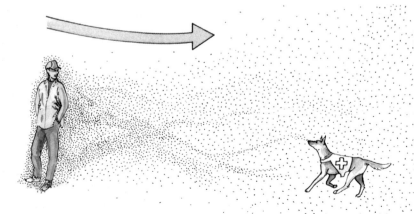

Air scent dogs work with their noses high to find scent as it is carried in the air directly from a person's body.

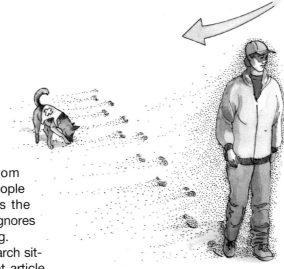

Trailing dogs follow scent from a person after it has settled on the ground. Over time, scent blows away from the person's path of travel.

is aware of scent from other animals and people in the area, it follows the assigned scent and ignores all others while working.

There are many search situations where a scent article may not be used, such as avalanche, water search, or urban disaster, to name a few. In fact, many wilderness search teams in the country do not require their air scent dogs to use a scent article in wilderness searches. In these situations, the dog finds the scent of any person in the area and finds their location. When the dog is asked to look for anyone on the search, the handler may want to keep the space as free of additional scent as possible by limiting the number of people in the area to be searched. Keeping the search areas clear of conflicting scent prevents too much contamination of the target scent, which would otherwise make the problem more difficult for the dog to resolve. An air scent dog can work an area that has been heavily contaminated by others after the air has been cleared of the immediate contamination, which

occurs naturally over time. If the missing person is still present in the area, the dog will be able to locate that person without scent discriminating. Air scenting and trailing are explained in greater detail in later chapters.

Dogs are predators and they have a natural drive to seek out and capture prey. This natural drive to hunt is especially valuable when used to search for missing people under adverse conditions. A good search dog uses its instinct to stay focused on its goal over time and distance. As will be further explained in a later chapter, a search dog is basically hunting for the lost individual by locating their scent and identifying where it's most intense, until the dog follows it to the person or captures its prey. Strong prey and hunt drives are essential traits in a search dog.

What Is a Dog Team?

A search dog team consists of a dog and handler who have achieved certification together in a particular search and rescue discipline. Certification is based on specific standards of achievement determined by search dog agencies throughout the nation. In most regions, wilderness search and rescue teams also include at least one support person or navigator for any mission. The navigator is usually assigned to the dog team at each mission, but the dog and handler train and usually live together. In fact, the working handler is usually responsible for training the dog because so much depends on the quality and strength of their partnership. Most search dogs are owned by and live with their handlers as members of the family, in addition to their duties as search dogs. Exceptions to this are *backup handlers,* who are included in some teams, although not all. Backup handlers are generally used in avalanche search work, although some wilderness teams also have provisions for backup handlers, and each handler must still certify with the dog as an individual dog team in order to work in actual missions.

Another valuable part of a dog team is the *support person.* Support people may be the navigator in the wilderness, the safety officer after an avalanche, or the medical officer in a disaster. These people do not necessarily need to be acquainted with the dog and handler, but they should definitely appreciate and respect dogs. They must also have the skills to do what is needed to support the dog team on a mission. The basic skills required of a support person include search and rescue techniques appropriate for the discipline, navigation using map and compass and/or a global positioning system (G.P.S.) device, and knowledge of radio communication. Anyone supporting a dog team must also be able to keep pace with the dog and handler while not interfering with the work. A good support person knows how to support, rather than lead the dog team.

Tracking dogs follow a person's path with their noses to the ground to detect bacteria in soil and vegetation that has been disturbed as a person walks.

Search dogs must be strong and agile to navigate around and through difficult terrain.

A Profile of the Handlers and Dogs

Search and rescue is a true labor of love for the people and dogs who spend so much of their time training and working together. People who respond to missions often volunteer their time, and commit to providing professional level expertise to each mission. They also usually hold full-time jobs in fields unrelated to emergency services, and dedicate their free time to training themselves in addition to training their dogs. Due to the requirements of the commitment, this hobby can easily become a second full-time job.

A good guideline for people who want to train a dog for search and rescue is that they should love working with dogs almost more than anything else. The reason is that handlers spend most of their free time focused on developing and enhancing their partnership with their dogs. Every experience for a search dog in-training and its handler should contribute to the dog's overall stability, and the team's confidence in any situation that may arise. Much of the dog's training happens during daily activities, such as going for a walk in the park to practice obstacles using the slide and the teeter-totter. People who work search dogs cherish the extremely close bonds they develop with their dogs, and love the work.

Everyone who gets involved in search and rescue also loves adventure. The dog team may be asked to rappel off a cliff face or drive a snowmobile into the wilderness. In fact, in wilderness search and rescue, teams may be deployed many miles into an unfamiliar and wild area to search in the middle of the night in the middle of a blizzard. For these and other

Disaster response dogs are trained to follow obedience commands across a variety of obstacles.

reasons, navigation skills using a map and compass and G.P.S. are mandatory in wilderness search and rescue. The dog and handler may be flown into a search area by helicopter and, even if the lost person is located and air lifted to safety, the dog team may need to hike many miles to get to a road where they can be picked up in a vehicle and returned to the command base.

Search dogs love to work and love working with their handlers. They're confident and trusting of their partnership. These dogs enjoy new and exciting situations and are able to stay calm while riding in a snowmobile, boat, or helicopter. Search dogs must also accept new dogs and strangers, and learn to work with many people yelling around them, helicopters, low-flying planes, generators, and all-terrain vehicles. In addi-

tion to the noises, search dogs work alongside the equipment and vehicles that contribute to the noise. Certainly, disaster response dogs are called on to work under conditions that are more extreme than most people can imagine.

Dog teams must be able to maintain their focus and continue to work through bad weather, difficult terrain, and extreme conditions. In the wilderness, people are usually reported missing after dark or after bad weather has come into the area. It's important for a dog team to be prepared for any situation. In the Rocky Mountains, a search that starts on a warm, clear day at the home where the person was last seen may quickly turn into a search at high altitude in freezing temperatures and blinding snow as darkness quickly approaches.

Some dogs are rewarded with food or toys and play at the end of a search, and some respond instead to the shared satisfaction of tracking down their quarry and completing their task. Although all search dogs do not respond to a reward of food or toys, rewards of some kind help keep the dogs' motivation high. Praise is always essential. Often the key element that inspires a dog and handler to continue to work is the reward of working together, as a team, to find someone who's lost, injured, or otherwise endangered. Most handlers feel that the service they provide with their dogs is the most valuable contribution they can offer.

Where Are Search and Rescue Dogs Used Effectively?

Dog teams are effective in a multitude of emergency situations and locations. Described as *just another resource* used in search and rescue by some people, they are, nevertheless, an extremely valuable resource. In fact, a trained search dog may be the most valuable search instrument in many situations. Search dogs are required to work in a broad range of emergency search situations that require specialized skills. Among the attributes that make search dogs so reliable are their physiology, natural drives, physical strength, and stamina. Search dogs can be trained across several specialties and have no problem making the transition when required.

Wilderness

In his book, *Wilderness Search and Rescue,* Tim J. Setnicka (Appalachian Mountain Club Books, 1981) says, "One trained search dog can patrol a tract in 6 hours that would take 106 workers 370 man-hours to comb with the same probability of detection." Wilderness search and rescue includes many situations that cover a variety of terrain and conditions. Using either trailing or air scenting techniques, a wilderness search may begin in a parking lot and move quickly into a field, the forest, the desert, or the mountains. In fact, since wilderness search training requires such a broad range of techniques, it provides an excellent basis for the other search specialties. A handler must realize that a search for a lost or missing person in the wilderness can turn into a water or avalanche search in many parts of the country, or incorporate locating evidence or searching through buildings.

Avalanche

Avalanche dogs are usually based in ski areas in order to provide the quickest and most accurate resource for locating people buried in avalanches. However, with the increasing popularity of backcountry skiing, snow boarding, and snowmobiling, dogs certified in avalanche now need to be available throughout larger areas in the mountains, not just in ski resorts. Avalanche dogs use air scent techniques and need to be

Many search dogs are trained to locate and identify anything belonging to a victim. These dogs must be able to discriminate a specific scent.

enthusiastic about digging in order to help the handler locate, and hopefully, rescue the buried person as quickly as possible.

Water

Water searches involve finding people who have drowned in either moving water, such as rivers, or still water, such as lakes, ponds, or canals. By identifying the scent in the air, dogs trained in water search may work along the shoreline or from a boat or canoe. These dogs are not necessarily expected to swim to the drowned victim. Instead, the dogs identify that the subject is in the water and can be invaluable in narrowing the search area for scuba divers who actually retrieve the body. Even if a search dog does not enjoy swimming, it needs to be able to swim in case it falls into the water, and should definitely enjoy being around water and in boats for water search.

Search dog handlers love their dogs and enjoy working with them for many hours every week.

Cadaver and Human Remains Detection

Although most search dogs are expected to find people who may have died recently, cadaver dogs are trained to look for and pinpoint the location of remains above and below ground. Human remains detection dogs and cadaver dogs are trained to detect scent from bodies, bones, and scattered remains that may have been buried for a long time. In addition to solid remains, cadaver dogs are used to locate forensic evidence, body fluids, and body parts. The areas worked may be either urban or wilderness. Remarkably, cadaver dogs can even detect scent from remains that have been buried several feet underground for many years.

Evidence

Search and rescue dogs are often required to locate objects thrown or dropped in an area during a crime. This evidence may be extremely valuable in solving a crime or convicting a criminal. Dogs trained in evidence detection search for anything that has absorbed human scent or is covered with the scent from a specific individual. Evidence techniques may be used in wilderness searches where the dog identifies an article dropped by the lost person, providing another clue that the person has been in the area.

Disaster/Urban

Dogs trained in disaster techniques have been more widely used over the past several years. The disasters may be naturally occurring or the result of bombs or large-scale attacks by humans. Federal disaster dogs are trained and certified under very specific standards established under the Federal Emergency Management Agency (FEMA). These standards include the ability to work amid rubble and debris quickly and safely while following commands and signals from the handler. Disaster response dogs certified under FEMA's standards look for live people buried in the rubble and must bark to alert the handler to their discovery. Other certification standards for disaster response dogs include looking for bodies or cadavers. Either way, the dog should be extremely athletic and agile in order to work safely under these conditions. A disaster response dog's response to obedience commands must be unfailing, given the dangerous conditions under which it works.

When and How Are Search and Rescue Dogs Deployed?

Certified dog teams are generally part of a network of search and rescue agencies connected through federal and/or local emergency services or law enforcement. As mentioned earlier, the handlers usually volunteer their time. When called, they often leave a job or a family to go to an unknown location for an unknown period of time to help someone

Search dogs and their handlers enjoy adventure. This dog team is prepared for anything.

who's become lost, injured, or worse. The specific procedures used to deploy these teams may vary depending on the area, but they do follow the same general guidelines.

As an example, typical searches in the mountains frequently involve missing children and adults whose health may be at risk. In these cases, someone notifies the local emergency services or sheriff's department, often simply by dialing 911. The sheriff's department then requests state or county search and rescue resources through their dispatching procedures. The sheriff's office then describes the situation to the search agency, including age, health, clothing, and physical

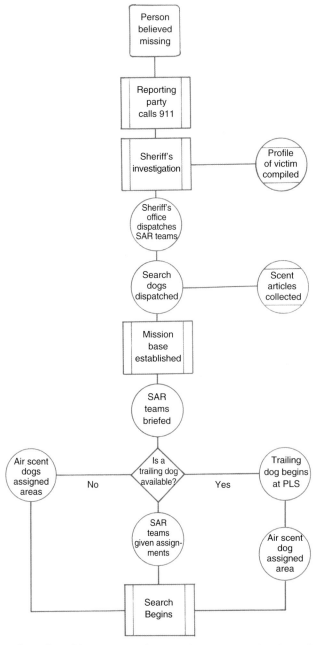

Person
believed
missing

Reporting
party
calls 911

Sheriff's
investigation

Profile
of victim
compiled

Sheriff's
office
dispatches
SAR teams

Search
dogs
dispatched

Scent
articles
collected

Mission
base
established

SAR
teams
briefed

Air scent
dogs
assigned
areas

No

Is a
trailing dog
available?

Yes

Trailing
dog begins
at PLS

SAR
teams
given assign-
ments

Air scent
dog
assigned
area

Search
Begins

Call out procedures for wilderness searches vary by groups and regions. Some search and rescue teams are dispatched through local emergency services.

condition of the lost person. When available, scent articles are collected as quickly as possible by a person trained in the methods used to collect articles. Search teams are dispatched and, if necessary, handlers may also collect the scent articles along the way to the mission, although this is not always possible in many situations. All the search teams first meet at the command base, where they are briefed and given their assignments.

Search and rescue efforts are coordinated among several agencies. Procedures vary depending on the situation, individual protocols, and/or resources. National, statewide, and local organizations work to establish guidelines and standards for search and rescue, including the use of dogs. Standardization of requirements and procedures enable teams around the nation and around the world to work together effectively and efficiently.

This explanation of search and rescue procedures and search and rescue dogs is meant to provide an overview for those interested in gaining an understanding of what's involved in training and working a

Avalanche dogs enjoy digging in snow. They are trained to dig toward the victim.

search dog. A list of resources is also included at the end of this book. Search and rescue requires that dog teams coordinate their efforts with other teams of trained personnel. Therefore, a handler's membership in a search and rescue agency is valuable in developing good knowledge and skills when working a dog in this field. With this understanding, it's now possible to go into greater detail about what makes a good search dog and what makes a good handler.

Chapter Two

The Dog Team

As described in the previous chapter, a dog team is comprised of the search dog and the dog's handler. It is important to note that the dog and handler are not merely individual members of the same team, but partners. A dog and handler share more than just experience. In fact, both the dog and handler each have special qualities, characteristics, and skills that are basic to canine search and rescue.

Qualities of a Search Dog

The word *quality* is being used here to describe one's essential nature, in this case the essential nature of the dog. Qualities of the dog can be nurtured, but are inherent, which means they already exist by the time search training begins. Qualities essential for a successful search dog are physical soundness, a stable temperament, and strong prey and hunt drives.

Physical Soundness

A dog working in search and rescue needs to be physically sound for several obvious reasons. The dog is required to have good hearing, excellent sight, and an acute sense of smell so that it can be fully aware of all stimuli while working. Many air scent dogs work beyond the range of their handler's sight, so good hearing and eyesight are invaluable because the dog must be able to either get back to the handler or keep the handler in sight and hearing range during both day and night searches and in bad weather. Of course, a good sense of smell is mandatory.

Also, it generally takes two to three years to certify a dog in the basic search and rescue disciplines, so it's best if the dog can spend several years actually working in the field once certified. If a dog is only sound for a few years, the time spent actually working is limited. This is only one of the reasons physical soundness is important. Structural soundness is also critical because search dogs work over varied and difficult terrain and obstacles for long periods of time. The dog needs to be able to climb, jump, swim, balance, and walk through diverse environments, climates, altitudes, and conditions.

Physical soundness, strength, and acute senses may be reinforced through a good nutritional and training program. The dog should be fed an appropriate, consistent, and balanced diet to maintain an optimal body weight. In addition, regular physical training is required to encourage strong muscles and bones. As with people, consistent physical activity is more effective than infrequent, sudden demands, even on a well-conditioned body.

Stable Temperament

A sound temperament is important for all dogs that work closely with people. Although each breed is characterized by its own distinct behavioral patterns, the general temperament should be stable and reliable. A dog with a sound temperament is playful, self-confident, curious, non-aggressive, responsive, and happy to socialize. Search dogs confront many new and often odd circumstances, generally working under very stressful conditions. A dog whose temperament is reliable continues to be an asset in every situation.

Building on a stable temperament, a search dog must become accustomed to noise, chaos, shouting, very active children, anxious people, and all manner of unusual situations without becoming over-excited or frightened. With a sound temperament as described here, a dog can be exposed to these situations in training and gain the confidence to continue to work through most circumstances as they arise during missions.

Strong Prey and Hunt Drives

Mentioned earlier is the fact that a search dog's drive to seek and find is based on the animal's natural instinct to hunt and track down prey. Prey drive refers to the dog's eagerness to chase or pursue and capture a fleeing target, such as a toy, an animal, or a person. Hunt drive describes the dog's willingness or desire to search out, follow, and find the scent of the prey. The instinct to hunt enables the dog to be diligent under all kinds of circumstances. A dog with strong prey and hunt drives may be well suited to search and rescue work, where the nature of the work can be long and arduous at times. Surprisingly, situations do arise in which the lost person may actually run from searchers, and the dog needs to keep working even when the subject appears to be getting away. In this circumstance, the source of the scent keeps moving away from the dog and the dog must stay focused in order to pinpoint the source's location.

Hunt drive is especially appreciated when the dog is required to dig or scratch to get closer to scent or its source. In situations where a dog is unable to achieve direct contact with the missing person, such as avalanches, disasters, or cadaver work, the dog may need to dig or bark to alert the handler to the location of the scent source (the prey).

Though instinctive, the drive to pursue and hunt prey can be nurtured and reinforced, as can the drive

A dog's willingness to search is based on strong, natural prey and hunt drives.

or desire to play. Games of retrieving, runaway, and hide-and-seek are fun for puppies and most adult dogs. These games also reinforce the desire to play and have fun with people and other dogs, which is important for a search dog. When formal search training begins, the dog will continue to draw on these inherent qualities to work through problems.

Characteristics of a Search Dog

Whereas the quality of a dog describes the essential nature of dogs, the *characteristics* of a dog is used here to describe the dog's traits, which may vary according to the particular dog. The dog's breed,

early socialization, responsiveness and reliability, and love of work are characteristics that all contribute to making a good search dog.

Breeds

Search and rescue dogs most commonly come from the herding, hunting, or working breeds, or from mixed breeds with the characteristics of these groups in their bloodlines. The dog's adult size and weight needs to be appropriate for the situations in which it is expected to work. In addition, dogs from these breed groups are generally predisposed to working with people. This is important not only because the dog works directly with the handler, but also works hard to find strangers.

Finally, when selecting a breed for search and rescue, a handler must be aware of his or her own preferences. Compatibility is key with a close partnership, and a handler should select a breed with which he or she can work well.

Socialization

In addition to the stable temperament already mentioned, a search dog must be very well socialized. The dog will spend all of its working life among people, both familiar and unknown, so socialization must be a priority. Socializing a puppy can include taking it into stores where dogs are allowed, to playgrounds, parks, airports, dog shows, and other situations where the puppy can have safe contact with many people and dogs. It's vital to give the dog in training a great deal of contact with children and other animals while maintaining its sense of security.

Responsiveness and Reliability

Working dogs must be responsive to their handlers. When dogs are responsive to their handlers, they are reliable partners. Search and rescue, by its nature, places the dog team in new and sometimes dangerous situations and, like people, few dogs are willing to remain in uncomfortable situations for long, much less continue to work in those situations. For this reason, it's imperative that the dog not be easily excited or frightened.

Reliability means the dog's behavior is consistent with the handler's expectations in any situation. For example, people are often reported missing during bad weather, so it's not unusual for a dog team to work during thunder and lightning. Under such conditions, the dog needs to stay calm, listen to and remain with the handler, and go back to work after the storm passes.

It's important to train under diverse conditions so that the dog team can learn to work efficiently in unusual circumstances. This variety builds each team member's confidence in one another and provides

Many dog breeds are used in search and rescue.

Search dogs must be able to interact amicably and share space with other dogs.

The dog's love of and desire to work is reinforced through positive training experiences and lots of play as reward. Ideally, a search dog's training is built on successful experiences and rewarded with praise, play, and/or food. Certainly, praise is always incorporated into the dog's reward. When placed in a position to succeed or win by getting to the prey during training, the dog will be thrilled when the handler's pager goes off and it's time to go to work.

Skills of a Search Dog

Whereas qualities are inherent and characteristics are distinguishing traits, skills are specific learned behaviors that enable a search dog to accomplish its job competently. Search dogs need to develop a specific set of skills in order to be effective in their discipline. In addition to the required search skills, social skills, obedience, and agility are basic for search dogs.

Social Skills

Being well socialized is a characteristic of search dogs, but social skills specifically describe what search dogs must learn in order to relate well to one another. The ability and willingness to interact with other dogs in a friendly manner is very important.

The pack social order of wild dogs also defines behavior among domestic dogs, which may be counter-

experience in handling the dog under stress. It also establishes the foundations of trust crucial to the success of the search and rescue dog team.

Love of Work

One reason a good search dog continues to work under stress is that, quite simply, the dog loves to work. Anyone who has an opportunity to watch a working dog do what it's trained to do is immediately impressed by the dog's focus. A dog that loves to work does so willingly and happily and doesn't need to be forced. Such dogs also work well under pressure and for extended periods of time. Search and rescue missions often last throughout the night and sometimes even days. For this reason alone, the dog needs to be eagerly anticipating working when it's responding to a mission.

productive to human social requirements. In search and rescue, a working dog must be able to sit in a truck or helicopter with other dogs without acting territorial. That willingness to share territory may also include searching areas that overlap or cross into another dog's assigned area. Disaster response dogs are often crowded together in a vehicle or plane when they travel to disaster sites.

In addition to sharing space, a search dog also needs to be able to share its *find* or prey with other dogs. Avalanche or disaster work requires that the dog making the initial discovery back out of the tight space where the subject is buried, enabling a second dog to move in to confirm the find. Because this is challenging to many dogs, they must be trained to accept the protocol.

The start of each training session with search dog teams should provide various opportunities for the dogs to play and socialize. If off-lead socialization is allowed, the dogs should be monitored for signs of dominant behavior, such as raised hackles or posturing, so the dominant dog can be calmly, but firmly, steadied. Given the opportunity, the dogs often work out their own understanding of their place in the pack and posturing may be avoided. Some search teams don't allow off-lead play among the dogs, so other means of socialization may include on-lead play and obedience training. However, this skill cannot be left to chance, so it needs to be part of the training process.

Obedience

Obedience is critical for a search dog and must be a priority. The safety of dog and handler could be at risk if a dog fails to respond to some of the most basic obedience commands. Mentioned earlier are basic commands, such as *come, sit, stay, down* and *heel,* that must be taught and reinforced regularly. Many more commands are incorporated as training progresses, as are hand signals. Because some search dogs work entirely off lead, obedience at a distance is equally critical. Disaster response dogs always work off lead and will often be sent to search through areas where people are unable to move easily. Dogs trained in avalanche rescue work entirely off lead, as do most dogs trained in wilderness search. In fact, as a general rule, only a trailing dog is worked on lead, and even many trailing dogs are worked off lead.

An obedient dog is able to work more independently than a dog that needs to be constantly monitored. In effect, obedience ultimately gives a dog more freedom because the handler has confidence in the dog's response. An important element of canine search and rescue is that the dog is often required to make decisions that can define the direction of the search. Therefore, when teaching obedience skills to a search and rescue dog, it's important to create the proper balance. The dog must feel confident enough to make decisions on its own, but be willing to look to the handler for direction and confirmation when needed.

A search dog learns to move easily and comfortably through tight spaces.

Agility

As with obedience, agility skills are also imperative for search dogs. A search dog needs to be able to navigate through challenging terrain. It must be able to climb into and out of narrow spaces or tunnels and balance in precarious situations. Although *agility* is the term used to describe this skill, training encompasses more than the basic agility course work commonly recognized for competition.

Instead of encouraging speed, as in agility competitions, the search and rescue dog must be precise and careful. A basic obstacle or disaster course consists of slides, ladders, wobbly bed springs, tunnels and teeter-totters, as well as broken and piled wood and concrete, jumbled and scattered tires, high beams, and cat walks. Well-trained search dogs are very athletic and generally enjoy these challenges as they gain confidence.

A disaster obstacle course is one means of teaching agility, but obstacles can be found in other situations as well. Climbing around large rocks and boulders, crossing logs, and working through downed timber in a forest are a few of the other training options. As with all other phases of training, it's important to build confidence and trust using positive reinforcement while keeping the dog safe.

Qualities of a Search Dog Handler

People sometimes forget that the handler is the other half of a good search and rescue dog team. The training may be focused primarily on the dog, but the handler's qualities, characteristics, and skills are also critical to the partnership. The qualities of a good handler include good physical health, mental stability, and a love of dogs.

Physical Health

Anyone who participates in search and rescue, with or without a dog, should be in adequate physical health to accomplish most assignments. In addition to the equipment required

Information gathered by search dogs may define the direction, course, or success of a mission. The handler understands this responsibility.

for basic search and rescue, dog handlers must also be able to carry enough gear, food, and water in their backpack to provide for themselves and the dog. Other rigorous physical demands include hiking through difficult terrain over long distances, possibly at high altitudes, and working in precarious and dangerous situations following a disaster.

Most search agencies require applicants to have medical clearance before joining, and some require their members to pass physical fitness tests. The handler needs to be strong enough to assist the dog when needed, by lifting it up and over obstacles. In addition, as a member of a search team, the dog handler must be able to help other team members if the subject of the search is found injured or dead. This could require assisting with guiding or carrying a litter down a cliff face or, mountainside, or lifting it over rocks on fairly steep terrain.

Sometimes the most challenging requirement for a handler is simply moving at a reasonable rate to keep pace with the dog while working. Of course, no dog handlers want to become a liability on a search mission because they're unable to keep up with their own dogs.

Mental Stability

People responding to search and rescue missions want to help others. Although generous and appreciated, helping is not always easy. By its very nature, search and rescue can be mentally and emotionally challenging. Some searches end in tragedy or are the result of a tragedy. Circumstances may leave many questions unanswered. The scenes witnessed by everyone following the attacks on the World Trade Center and the Pentagon are the most extreme examples of what dog handlers may have to deal with when responding to a mission. Dog teams, in particular, tend to attract attention on searches, in the form of high expectations or demands. Therefore, the dog handler needs to be aware of his or her own emotional reaction in every situation.

A good dog handler should know that the information gathered by the dog might define the search and the direction it takes. Because handlers need to rely on the dog's guidance, they must allow the dog to take the lead. This can be difficult if the handler is someone who believes he or she needs to be in control at all times. Working a search dog can be very humbling, even for the best dog handlers.

A dog handler needs to be able to work alone and in groups. Generally the dog team searches somewhat in isolation from other members of an agency. Rather than going into the wilderness as part of a team of three or more people, as is common with search agencies that don't specialize in canine search and rescue, a dog team's assignment separates them from others. At the same time, a good handler is able to work with people who may not always under-stand or agree with the way a search is progressing.

There are also times when a dog team's methods or information is questioned, which may be challenging. Few people who don't also work dogs are aware of the wealth of information that a dog team collects during a search. Although it's appropriate to question the information received, it can be difficult when the questions appear to challenge the handler's or the dog's knowledge or capabilities. A good handler needs to respond appropriately and unemotionally to questions such as, "How do you know?" "Are you sure?" "What do you recommend?" or the comment, "That can't be right!"

Loves Dogs

It's valuable to emphasize that search dog handlers spend a large amount of their time with their dogs. Training, practice sessions, and actual missions generally occupy most of their free time. For this reason, dog handlers should love dogs and love working with their particular dog.

One aspect of this is the enjoyment of the whole process of discovering the unique nature of the dog's capabilities, which may not always match what the handler envisioned for the team. For example, a dog may work slower and more methodically than the handler had expected. Someone who enjoys working with dogs is willing to adjust to the different style and to learn to work in a new way in order to complement the dog's abilities.

Characteristics of a Search Dog Handler

Certain characteristics make a dog handler a valuable resource in search and rescue. These traits include a love of adventure, working well under pressure, and reliability.

Love of Adventure

Search and rescue teams are generally comprised of individuals who enjoy adventure. Handlers can never really know what they'll face when they respond to a mission, and must be willing to take some calculated risks. Skills and effective training enable a dog team to face most situations with confidence. It's important to understand that not every search ends in success. In fact, each new situation becomes an exciting challenge and an experience to use as a model for future training. Search and rescue dog handlers enjoy this challenge, and look forward to each new experience.

Working Well Under Pressure

A dog handler needs to be able to make decisions and work well under pressure. This pressure can take the form of physical barriers to be overcome, or it may be of an emotional nature. While everyone who works in search and rescue is faced with this pressure, a dog handler must stay calm and steady for the sake of the dog. Whether the dog team continues to work or the handler needs to stop working to discuss a distressing situation while the dog waits, it is the handler's responsibility to be aware of the effect this response has on their dog.

A good way to prepare for this pressure is to work with an agency that can set up mock searches under a variety of circumstances. As with other challenging endeavors, practice is important. Other team members can provide insight and are valuable sources of constructive criticism and support in these situations.

Reliability

A search dog handler is generally expected to be available most of the time. Because emergency situations are unexpected, search dog handlers rarely know when or to what extent they'll be needed. When a dog team responds to a mission, they need to be available for the duration of their assignment.

Reliability extends to the dog team's ability to work on the specific problem. Reliable handlers are able to say whether their dog's experience is appropriate for each problem. They also need to be willing to decline an assignment when it's too dangerous for the team.

One of the jobs of the handler is to report the dog's findings back to mission base. They need to be as accurate and as succinct as possible when discussing the search with the mission authorities or incident command. A handler who provides reliable information is one who reports

A search dog waits patiently while his handler reports to mission base.

facts that can contribute to an effective outcome, rather than one who simply speculates.

Skills of a Search Dog Handler

Search dog handlers train their own dogs and, in doing so, share their knowledge with their dogs. As with the dog, the handler has an extensive set of skills learned over time. The basic skills dog handlers

need include knowledge about mission protocol, the skills required for their particular specialty, and, sometimes overlooked in training, first aid.

Mission Protocol

Mission protocol refers to the processes and procedures used during a search and rescue incident. While dog handlers don't need to know how to manage an incident, they do need to have a working knowledge of the basic procedures to be followed. Examples are where to report when the team first arrives, the behavior expected while working, and how and to whom to report findings. A dog team is a valuable resource, but it's one of several tools used in search and rescue, and the handler needs to understand this to work within the expected protocols. One way to learn about mission protocol is to join and participate in a search agency's activities. Dog teams are most often called by other agencies, and dog handlers can become familiar with search and rescue protocols through their own participation.

Specialty

Dog handlers need to be well versed in the requirements of their particular specialty. Many unique skills are required for each of the search and rescue specialties even before the dog gets involved. For example, in wilderness search and rescue, basic map and compass, mountaineering and rock climbing skills, and awareness of rescue techniques are necessary. Avalanche rescue work involves experience in snow travel and an understanding of the mechanics of avalanche. Disaster response dog handlers are required to learn about hazardous materials and contamination, and other information they would likely need when responding to missions. Each of the other disciplines has their own special basic skill requirements. A good amount of time and effort goes into learning and refining these skills, in addition to training the dog.

As with mission protocol, the best way to learn these special skills is to get involved with an agency or team specializing in the specific area of interest. Once learned, it's also valuable to continue to update the knowledge.

Search missions are often challenging and a search dog handler may need to assist other team members.

First Aid

Training and certification in advanced first aid or first responder are minimum mandatory requirements for many emergency service agencies. The Red Cross and other agencies usually sponsor training in first aid techniques in all regions. Equally important is knowledge of first aid for dogs. Techniques used to administer first aid to dogs can be quite different from those applied to humans. If the dog becomes injured in an area where immediate assistance is unavailable, the handler may be the only person who can stabilize the dog's condition. Veterinarians who are knowledgeable about canine emergency services are valuable resources for learning first aid techniques for dogs.

These qualities, characteristics, and skills are essential elements of a good search dog team and they are integral to the effectiveness of the partnership. These principles also provide the foundation for understanding the operation and mechanics of canine search and rescue. The ability to master them determines the effectiveness and success of the search dog team.

Chapter Three

Getting Started

When someone considers actually training a search dog, one of the first questions most people ask is, "What does it take?" People who want to train a dog for search and rescue should know what's involved before making the commitment. Training a search dog through the certification process requires a real investment of time, training, travel, and money. Understanding the considerations for selecting the right dog for the team is equally important.

Time

It takes a great deal of time for a dog team to become a trained, valuable resource. Agencies involved in search and rescue dog training usually hold weekly training sessions. Participating in these sessions is valuable for learning and sharing knowledge, skills, and experience. In addition to weekly group training during the first year, the dog team should practice their lessons three to six days a week. This schedule continues throughout the first year of training. A first year practice session can last anywhere from one to three hours, depending on the scenarios set up for the dog. After the first year of training it's possible to practice two to three times each week, and this may include training with the whole group.

Initially, training and practice sessions are designed around meeting the requirements for certification. Depending on the particular discipline, certification in wilderness search disciplines can take 18 months to 3 years. However, once certified, it's still important for the dog team to continue to practice at least a few times each month, in addition to responding to missions. Regularly scheduled practice sessions help maintain the dog's skill level and give the handler the opportunity to see how well the dog is functioning between missions. They also provide a controlled setting in which the team can work on problems encountered during actual missions.

Search missions may occur frequently or sporadically, depending on the area and the season. In some parts of the country search missions occur only occasionally and in others they can be frequent during particular seasons. In ski country, an avalanche dog team may respond to multiple avalanches in a short period of time, depending on the conditions of the snow. It's possible for a dog team to be called several times during one week, and only occasionally for the rest of the season. When training for disaster search, handlers should understand that they might continue to train for several years beyond certification before being called to a mission. The enjoyment of working a search dog should be its own reward, because the majority of the time working a search dog is spent training, not on missions.

The time required to search on missions also varies. A team may drive several hours to a mission to find they're only needed for a short period of time or that they're no longer needed at all. Missions can also last several days. The amount of time a dog team must commit to a mission may also be determined by circumstances, which only become clear after the team starts searching. These possibilities need to be understood when time is a consideration and, once understood, can generally be less frustrating than when a handler is expecting to be deployed frequently and on every mission.

Training

Training for search and rescue is multi-faceted and continues throughout the dog team's career. Actual

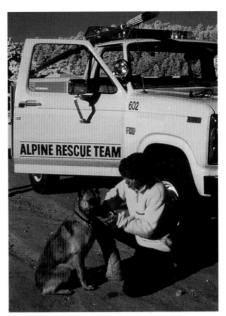

Search dog handlers become familiar with and follow mission protocols as they prepare to search.

search and rescue training is completely experiential for both dog and handler, and should build on a team's strengths over time. Mentioned earlier is the fact that working a search dog requires a handler to be a knowledgeable member of the search and rescue community at large—knowledge that is gained by training consistently within that community.

Although the overall training requirements are the same for all dog teams, some criteria vary depending on the techniques being taught. The two basic scenting techniques used by the dogs in search and rescue (described earlier) are trailing and air scenting. To review, when the dog works with its nose low following residual scent that has been deposited on the ground where a person has walked, the dog is trailing. When a dog identifies a person's or article's scent in the air as it is carried directly from the person's current location, the dog is air scenting. Dogs are trained to use either technique, and most dogs rely on both at various times while working. Although both of these techniques are used in wilderness search and rescue, air scenting alone is used for avalanche, water, and cadaver work.

The Environment

Training and practice sessions should be held in areas that simulate real working conditions. The initial problems that are set up for the beginning dog should be relatively simple, short, and straightforward. As training progresses, so should the complexity of the problems and the size of the area required to set up realistic search scenarios.

Trailing dogs require training exercises that combine distance and terrain complexity. The trailing dog works toward a goal of searching over several miles, across streams, through forests, fields and buildings, and around rocks or any other features that might be encountered on a mission.

A dog trained to air scent needs to work in areas that match its specialty. These areas should be large enough to challenge the dog while pinpointing the source of the scent among and through complex features, such as buildings, rubble piles, rocks, water, and trees.

Preparing the Site

Preparing each training and practice site requires planning and coordination. At least one person is required to hide or act as the missing person (the *subject*). For wilderness search training, the subject hiding for a trailing problem needs to hike a distance in a pattern that challenges the dog, yet also allows the dog to succeed. As the dog progresses in training, so should the age and difficulty of the subject's trail. At some point, the trail will need to be walked, or the *scent aged,* overnight or several days before the dog must work out the problem.

Wilderness air scent problems generally require less preliminary coordination, but still require planning. The subject for an air scent problem hikes to a location just before the dog is scheduled to work. An advanced air scent dog should be able to work a complex problem in a large area, so the person acting as the missing subject must be able to get to a location within that large area. Of course, each of the other specialties has particular training requirements as well.

There are many challenges to creating and maintaining a training area for disaster work, where potentially dangerous obstacles must be simulated and training areas need to be arranged. Disaster search training may be set up in collapsed structures, rubble piles, and salvage yards where the dog becomes accustomed to the environment of debris, odd smells, loud noises, and heavy equipment. The missing subject needs to hide in a location where the dog is challenged to carefully navigate to the source of the scent, so preplanning is involved when shoring up the debris to keep the dog, handler, and subject safe.

When training a dog for the agility element of disaster, it's necessary to set up a course that can be adjusted to provide the dog with dynamic experiences. The variety helps prepare the dog for the various situations the dog team will face in disaster search. The obstacle or agility course may include planks and ladders set at different angles, bed springs, boxes or cabinets, stacks of old tires, pipes or tubes, platforms, barrels, and anything else that simulates a jumble of obstacles or a collapsed building.

Coordinated planning and preparation are also needed when training a dog for avalanche, where the dog must learn to ride a chair lift, sled, and snowmobile, and detect people and articles buried under several feet of snow. When training a dog where there are skiers, or when using the ski resort's equipment, it's always necessary to first obtain clearance from the ski area. For the search scenarios to simulate avalanche debris fields as accurately as possible, the training areas must be pre-

An avalanche dog rides a chairlift up the mountain with its handler to report to work for the day.

pared well in advance of the actual training. Pits and/or caves must be dug in the snow, where the people acting as buried victims can hide. After the hiding areas are created, all the snow on the hillside also must be disturbed by side stepping along the slope in skis or snow shoes to prevent the dog from visually identifying the burial sites. Even the location of the snow caves must be planned in advance to accommodate more than one burial victim for a single exercise, or for multiple dogs to search in separate areas.

Although preparing the actual area is not as time consuming for water search training, there are a lot of details that must be addressed. To begin with, permission to use a body of water to work must be arranged with park services or whoever owns the land where the water is located. In addition to gaining permission to work in a lake or river, boats must be supplied, as well as scuba divers and/or cadaver material containing human scent, such as hair or teeth. Markers or buoys are also needed to train a water search dog, as well as a good helper who's able to maneuver the boat into the best position possible to support the dog's and handler's learning process.

Cadaver search, or human remains detection training, requires the material needed to create the source of the scent. This can be from hair, teeth, human bones, blood, other body fluids, or tissue. The integrity of the material must be kept viable by storing it in an airtight container in a refrigerator or freezer, or even leaving it at room temperature to continue the decaying process. The material should only be handled with gloves and special procedures must be followed in order to obtain the cadaver material in the first place. In addition to the human remains needed for training, areas used to hide the remains can include buildings, cars, fields, dirt piles, and stacked objects. All this requires planning.

Despite the challenges of creating a realistic training area, a creative handler can take advantage of training opportunities by finding facilities and areas where scenarios can be set up quickly. In fact, training opportunities are virtually unlimited for search dogs. Taking a search dog on a walk through an airport, where there's a tremendous amount of noise, activity, and general chaos, is only one possibility. Another might be to find an abandoned (but safe) building where there's debris that enhances unusual patterns of airflow for air scent problems. Whether in a formal training situation or a casual setting at the park or the playground, each experience should enhance the connection between the dog and handler as they learn more about each other.

Certification

Certification qualifies a search dog team to respond to actual missions in the region. The process of certification involves a series of tests that are designed to measure the capabilities of the dog and the handler based on specific standards. These standards may be developed directly from regulations at the local, state, or national level. While certification depends on the outcome of the tests, the quality of the dog team's partnership and the handler's knowledge and strategy are also evaluated when determining a dog team's effectiveness. Standards and testing procedures help assure an agency that the responding dog teams are qualified. They are also valuable tools for handlers to objectively measure their own effectiveness as a resource.

Once certified, a dog team may respond to missions as often as they are requested and available, although the dog teams may decide whether or not to respond with each mission. In other words, certification does not require that a volunteer search dog team respond to every mission for which they're called. However, given that search dogs are such valuable resources, it's often difficult to refuse to respond when needed.

Travel

Search dog teams often travel many miles to train and respond to missions. Because it's rare to find a good mixture of opportunities and people locally, most handlers are willing to go as far as necessary to train with other dog teams. In fact, the dynamic nature of search and rescue offers plenty of opportunities for a dog team to become familiar with many methods of transportation.

Private vehicles must be well maintained and built to handle the terrain in the region, whereas public transportation requires both training and documentation. In addition to traveling to practice and training, a dog team must often travel several hours, or even through the night to respond to a mission. For this reason, it's important to have reliable transportation, and the vehicle needs to be large enough to carry the dog, handler, search gear, and additional food and water. In some areas of the country, four-wheel drive is mandatory for search and rescue team responses in both the summer and winter.

The amount and type of travel involved with search and rescue requires that the dog be comfortable with a variety of transportation methods. When traveling longer distances to a search dog event (such as a training seminar, conference, test, or an actual emergency), search dogs may fly accompanied in the passenger section of an aircraft when permitted by the air carrier. Of course, the dog must be well behaved at all times, as flights may be fairly long. Dogs who use public transportation are required to have appropriate documentation, such as a health certificate. In addition, most airlines require accompanying identification specifying that the dog is traveling

A search dog and his handler ride together in the passenger section on a commercial flight to a search conference.

Search dog teams are often deployed in helicopters. The dogs and handlers need to be familiar with flight safety before embarking on their first mission.

for official search and rescue business, including training functions.

It's not unusual for dog teams to meet at a central location for training or missions, and ride together in a single vehicle, such as a bus or truck. This emphasizes the need for the dogs to be well behaved and willing to share space. The dogs may either be crated or sit side by side in close proximity to other dogs during what may be a long trip.

Another method of getting into a search area is by helicopter. Often, helicopter pilots will not transport individuals unless they've been trained in helicopter safety and protocol. Many search agencies provide training in loading and unloading while the helicopter's blades turn (a

hot load). It's important for the dog to be familiar with a helicopter and to offer no resistance during the loading process, sit quietly during the flight, and get to work immediately after disembarking. Of course, the handler's attitude and response is also important in conveying confidence to the dog.

Expenses

When considering the expenses of search and rescue, keep in mind that the initial outlay only needs to match the immediate requirements. It's not necessary to buy everything needed to support a career in search and rescue until it's actually required.

Costs incurred for the initial expenditure for search and rescue include outdoor gear, clothing, travel costs, vehicle maintenance, and training. Of course, these expenses are in addition to the cost of maintaining a healthy, happy, working dog.

To start with, a handler needs relatively high-quality outdoor and rescue equipment, or *gear,* that is reliable and won't fall apart at critical moments. Basic gear for wilderness search and rescue includes a backpack, water bottles, sleeping bag, climbing harness, helmet, a few sets of gloves, maps, and a two-way radio. Items referred to as *the ten essentials* of outdoor trekking are important to have; they are a compass, flashlight/headlamp, extra batteries, tarp or tube tent, extra clothing, sunglasses and sunscreen, extra food and water, waterproof matches and candle or fire starter, pocket knife, and first aid kit.

The type and quality of clothing can be critical. Clothing must be made for outdoor recreation, from fabric specifically designed for the temperatures and climates to be encountered. Good leather hiking boots with lug soles are essential, even in the summer months. Winter conditions have their own requirements for equipment, in addition to the items already mentioned. It's not uncommon to spend well over $3,000 when buying basic outdoor gear for the first time. Some agencies have an inventory of special equipment and may provide some or all of the equipment for their team

The Ten Essentials of Outdoor Trekking

Compass
Flashlight/Headlamp
Extra Batteries
Tarp or Tube Tent
Extra Clothing
Sunglasses and Sunscreen
Extra Food and Water
Waterproof Matches and Candle
   or Fire Starter
Pocket Knife
First Aid Kit

members. When this is the case, many dog handlers, and other search personnel, usually prefer to buy their own gear so they can be sure they have the correct equipment for all searches, whether or not they're searching with their own team. Also, owning the equipment gives handlers peace of mind in that they know everything fits or works well for them.

Basic equipment for the dog includes a non-restrictive harness, rappelling harness, search and rescue jacket or vest, collar, long lead and leash, toys, and travel bowls. Dog booties should also be included for some search situations. If booties are used, the dog should train in these before being asked to wear them in an actual search situation. Another important note is that search and rescue dogs do not wear panniers or saddlebags because they need to be able to move comfortably and freely in underbrush, buildings, and debris. Like the handler's equipment, the

Basic Gear for Handlers and Dogs

Handler's Basic Equipment	Handler's Winter Equipment	Canine Equipment
Backpack	Special Snow Boots	Collar
Water Bottles	Warm Hat	I.D.
Sleeping Bag	Balaklava	Non-Restrictive Harness
Climbing Harness	Mittens and Liners	Rappelling Harness
Helmet	Snow Proof Outerwear	6-Foot Lead
Leather Gloves	Down Jacket	30-Foot Lead
Maps	Avalanche Beacon*	SAR Vest
Radio	Avalanche Shovel	Dog Booties
Ten Essentials of Outdoor Trekking	Goggles	Toys
Hiking Boots	Skis and/or Snow Shoes	Travel Bowls
Waterproof Clothing	Probe-Type Ski Poles*	Light Sticks or Light
Synthetic Long Underwear		
Extra Socks		
Hat		
Jacket		
Closed Cell Pad**		

*For avalanche-prone areas
**As a barrier against the effects of lying or sitting on cold ground.

dog's gear must be high quality and well maintained. Food and water should always be carried for both the dog and the handler.

Travel expenses must be factored into the cost of search and rescue as well. The need for reliable transportation large enough to carry everything comfortably has already been mentioned. The additional costs associated with four-wheel drive vehicles should be added in some regions. The cost of gas and maintenance should also be considered, because travel may be far and frequent.

Details of travel are described in a previous section of this chapter.

The period needed to train a dog for certification can be used to test various brands and types of equipment and to determine what is actually needed. In addition to spreading out the costs, it gives handlers the opportunity to learn what works best for them. Advice from other search dog handlers can serve as guidance when selecting equipment, as well. However, first-hand experience generally proves to be the most valuable when selecting personal equipment.

The Dog

Of all the many considerations associated with search and rescue, the most important should be the dog. The dog is also the most important investment a handler makes. Dogs best suited for search and rescue generally come from the working, sporting, or herding breeds. Whatever the breed or combination of breeds, the dog needs to possess the qualities described in the previous chapter.

The adult dog's size, weight, and temperament should be appropriate for the demands of the job. These characteristics, as well as the working style of the particular breed, should be considered when selecting a breed. For example, some breeds are known to have an excellent ability to detect and follow scent but may be too large to work in the debris of a collapsed building following an earthquake. Other breeds, such as Greyhounds, are known for their speed and intensity, yet lack the quality and density of coat to work in snow for long periods and would be inappropriate as avalanche dogs.

Another consideration is whether the dog's personality is compatible with the specific working style of the handler. A handler who tends to work in a steady, methodical fashion while analyzing the details of a search works best with a dog that can reflect that style. The dog chosen should match the handler's profile. Breeds known for working exuberantly to cover large areas while running, such as some hunting breeds, would not be the most compatible when matched with the working style of the methodical handler just described.

Adult Dogs

Some dogs begin search and rescue training as adults. An advantage to this may be that their personality is already established, as is their relationship with the handler. An adult dog has also matured beyond the developmental phases of a puppy and can concentrate for longer periods of time. This maturity makes it possible for an adult dog to tackle

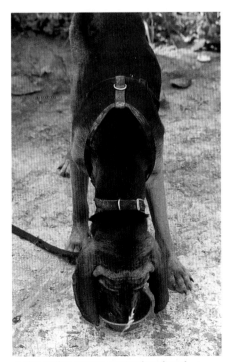

A flat collar, water, water bowl and harness is standard equipment for a trailing dog.

more complex problems earlier in training.

By the time a dog is considered an adult, its physical structure is also established. Because a search dog's capacity to work depends on a strong physical structure, it is an asset when the dog in training is known to be physically sound with good hips, elbows, and shoulder joints—all of which are critical to a dog working free of pain.

A drawback to training an adult dog is the relatively shorter amount of time the dog will spend actually working. Compared to a puppy, once certified, an adult dog will have fewer years to devote to actual missions before retiring. For this reason, some canine search teams limit the age of a dog they will accept for training toward certification. The reasoning is that the years of training aren't justified by the few years of work they can get from an older dog, so a five-year-old adult may be considered too old to begin training. This varies from team to team, and some dog handlers prefer to learn about training a search dog using their mature, seasoned adult dog so they'll be better informed when they start to train a puppy.

Puppies

Puppies can begin search and rescue training as early as eight weeks of age. As with an adult dog, the puppy needs to be bonded to the handler before formal training begins. An advantage of starting with a puppy is that the handler can provide the all-important socialization and obedience. Puppies learn quickly, but, normal developmental stages of growth and maturity may determine how quickly training can progress. Puppies tend to remain very receptive to search and rescue training throughout their maturity.

It's possible to incorporate specific temperament tests for search work along with the other temperament tests that are generally done at seven weeks of age. Many breeders use temperament tests to evaluate the puppy's personality. Temperament tests are helpful in measuring working drive and personality in puppies and can be valuable to handlers who know what they want. It's helpful for any handler to have a basic idea of the puppy's temperament, although any test should be considered a guide and not a final authority.

The Puppy Aptitude Test (P.A.T.) developed by Jack and Wendy Volhard (*Dog Training for Dummies,* IDG Books, 2001) can be found at *www.volhard.com.* This test was created to measure several criteria that can help determine a puppy's personality potential and basic responses as a prospect for a pet. The results of the test are measured using a scale from one to six to evaluate the puppy's responses.

The P.A.T. measures social attraction to people, the puppy's confidence and willingness to follow a person, and the degree of acceptance of social dominance by a person, also referred to as *pack drive.* It also measures degree of dominance or submission and the ease with which the puppy can be handled in a difficult situation. These criteria are referred to as *fight or flight drive,* as are the puppy's willingness to accept dominance by a person while it is in a position of no control and the degree to which the puppy startles when a strange object is placed near the puppy. The puppy's willingness to retrieve an object is used as a measure for *prey drive,* which can be an indication of degree of ease or difficulty in training, when measured with social attraction. Prey drive is also measured in this test by degree of sensitivity to sound and sight. Sensitivity to touch is also measured. The puppy's physical structural integrity is also evaluated in this test, because good structure is important for a healthy, happy dog and certainly for a working dog.

The tests are a meant as a guide when selecting a puppy for a pet. The same guides are helpful when selecting a puppy for a search and rescue dog, because basic tests that evaluate a future partner are better than guessing whether a puppy will be happy as a search dog.

The PAWS Working Dog Evaluation stands for Possessiveness, Attention, Willingness, and Strength, and was developed by J. Decker to assist in evaluating suitable "working" temperaments for dogs. It can be used along with the information gathered through the P.A.T. already described. This PAWS test can be used on older puppies as well as those who are seven weeks of age.

The size of a search dog is an important consideration. Courage and a big heart aren't always enough.

Instead of numeric scores, this test uses "Excellent," "OK," or "Indifferent" as measurements of the puppy's response.

Prey drive is evaluated using a teaser or toy appropriate for the age of the puppy, thrown a short distance. The puppy should run to the toy and either pick it up to "kill" it or check it out. The test for retrieve also uses a teaser or toy, which is thrown for the puppy to retrieve; it should either bring the toy back to the tester or return with it but want to continue to play. This test can also show the tester how engaging the puppy is likely to be with people or toys.

The tester can measure the puppy's hunt drive by tucking the toy under a foot while encouraging the puppy to find it. At the same time, the tester observes how persistently the puppy works to get the toy. A tug toy is used to evaluate the puppy's

The choice of training an adult dog or a puppy for search and rescue is based on a number of considerations.

tug response, possessiveness, and strength. The puppy can be encouraged to grab the tug toy, and should grab it and tug or just grab the toy. When the tester lets go of the toy, the puppy may either shake to "kill" it, try to get the tester to grab it again or shake the toy and run away. It's considered "OK" for the puppy to run away with the toy and drop it soon after.

Recall is tested for puppies older than three months of age, and a puppy younger than three months is tested for its willingness to follow a person. The recall test requires a helper to hold the puppy while the tester runs backward and calls the puppy once. The following test simply requires the tester to jog backward while clapping his or her hands together softly, encouraging the puppy. The puppy should run or trot to the tester and make an

effort to receive affection or continued attention.

Puppies have short attention spans relative to adult dogs, but this can also be measured. Attention is measured when the tester solicits the puppy's attention using a toy to achieve eye or facial contact from the puppy for 30 seconds. It's considered "Excellent" if the puppy watches the tester's face for the whole 30 seconds or briefly looks away, then back at the tester's face if there are other distractions. It's "OK" if the puppy needs to be re-engaged a few times. This test and more information about the process can be found at *www.malinut.com.*

The Brownell-Marsolais Scale: A Proposal for the Quantitative Evaluation of SAR/Disaster K9 Candidates, by David A. Brownell and Mark Marsolais, describes a screening test designed for use during the process of selecting a dog for search and rescue. Although designed specifically for disaster response dog candidates older than 12 months of age, the tests can be used to evaluate dogs being considered for any of the canine search and rescue disciplines. The authors of this series of screening tests believe strongly that a candidate dog needs to exhibit the right combination of drives and nerve strength in order to be successful in search and rescue, regardless of the results of other temperament screening tests.

There are six drives evaluated in this test. The first is the dog's ability to interact with a group of dogs or people, referred to as the *social* or *pack* drive. *Prey* drive, defined in an earlier chapter as the dog's desire to chase or capture prey, is also evaluated. *Hunt* drive, also mentioned earlier, is the dog's ability or desire to search for the prey using its nose when the prey is not visible. *Play* drive is defined as the dog's ability to interact with others in an entertaining manner, and is considered essential for training and easing stress during training and search missions. *Hunger* is measured to gauge how effective food motivation will be during training. The dog's drive to *defend* prey or *fight* to protect itself or the handler is also considered, although this behavior must be kept under control at all times. At the same time, when responding to a disaster or any search situation, a dog must be able to be removed from its find or prey and not refuse to relinquish control. Sometimes referred to as *victim loyalty,* a dog with steady fight drive is also able to work very hard and long to get to the scent source.

The authors of the tests, David Brownell and Mark Marsolais, describe nerve strength as ". . . a canine's ability to deal with or adapt to stress-producing environmental stimuli." This is also an important attribute to be measured in the test. Partly determined by breeding and genes, nerve strength can be encouraged through socialization and exposure to various stimuli throughout a dog's life. A search dog must be able to adapt to tremendous variety in its surroundings. The stimuli used to evaluate nerve strength in this test include *tactile,* which is a dog's ability to adapt to different and unstable surfaces as well as tight spaces; *aural,* which is the dog's ability to remain calm when exposed to loud noises, such as machinery, banging, pounding, and gunfire; and *visual,* which determines whether the dog can be trained or socialized to continue working when it encounters collapsed structures, heavy equipment, smoke, and large groups of people. The tests are mapped out clearly and scored according to the measurements defined on the scale. It's important to note that this test is intended for dogs over the age of 12 months and should not be performed on young puppies.

Another particularly useful test for a search dog is designed to measure a puppy's ability to detect scent. At seven weeks of age, a puppy is placed in an outdoor area where a small piece of meat has been hidden nearby. The tester observes how long it takes the puppy to detect the smell of meat and what it does after that. A good response for a potential search dog is for the puppy to quickly detect the scent, work diligently to locate the meat, and get to it in a relatively short period of time. This test can also offer a clue as to how the puppy solves problems. For a description of other possible criteria for selecting a puppy for search and rescue, go to *www. sardaa/puppy.htm.*

There are three additional points to keep in mind when selecting a puppy for search and rescue work. The first point is that temperament tests are meant to be used as a guide and may not be definitive. The second point is that when raising and training a puppy for search and rescue, or anything, the main responsibility rests on the owner and handler. The final point is that if the puppy selected exhibits high working drives and the new owner decides he or she no longer wants to pursue or continue search and rescue, the owner may be left with a very inquisitive, intelligent, and active dog that will look for something to do on its own. This may cause problems for the owner who is no longer able to challenge the puppy on the same activity level for which the puppy was selected.

Early Socialization

Whether beginning with an adult dog or a puppy, early socialization is vital to a dog's confidence. Socializa-

An avalanche dog must be well-suited to and enjoy working in the snow.

tion should include going to many public places. Airports and stores where dogs are allowed offer good experiences. Parks and playgrounds where there are many people and children also provide good experiences. The dog should be encouraged with a reassuring voice, but not forced into anything. Though possibly reticent at first, most dogs take cues from their owners and are willing to approach strangers even when they're feeling anxious.

Early socialization should always occur under controlled and safe conditions. This not only provides exposure to particular experiences, but enables the dog to gain confidence in various situations. Also, the dog learns to trust the handler when presented with unfamiliar situations. Reassurance from the handler also increases a dog's or a puppy's willingness to forge ahead to complete the job. Once formal training begins, a well-socialized dog or puppy can focus on the immediate tasks without requiring constant reassurance. There will always be new experiences for the puppy or dog, but the dog will have gained enough confidence to simply make the necessary adjustments and proceed with the work.

Choosing the right dog for the job can greatly ease the process of developing an effective team. At the same time, a good training program is vital in providing the tools and developing the skills that enable the dog team to excel in their chosen area of interest.

Chapter Four

Scent Dynamics

Although search dog handlers may have various reasons for being involved in search and rescue, it's important for all handlers to understand the nature of their job. In the most basic terms, the search dog handler must support the search dog at all times on a search and place the dog in the most likely position to succeed. Placing the dog in a position to succeed requires an understanding of what's happening for the dog during the search and what the dog needs to successfully follow through with the job. Likewise, developing a good search and rescue training program begins with a clear understanding of the nature of scent, the seach dog's tool.

What Are They Looking For?

The obvious answer to the question, "what are you looking for on a search?" is, "The lost person." Although finding the lost person is the ultimate goal of a search mission, what the dog team is really seeking is the path and the source of a particular scent. Scent may be influenced by many factors, such as wind, weather, temperature, humidity, and terrain. In order to understand what search dogs are doing, it's necessary to understand the nature of scent and its influences.

The nature of scent must first be reviewed before going further into its dynamics. People shed dead skin cells all the time. These skin cells are referred to as *rafts*. Skin rafts are continually being sloughed off wherever a person sits, stands, sleeps, or travels, and on anything a person touches. For a dog, each person's skin cells carry uniquely characteristic information, called *scent*. Skin rafts remain viable even in water. Dogs' wonderful physiology gives them the ability to detect these skin rafts even when they're heavily diluted by air or water. The bacteria that grow on skin cells create a vapor that enshrouds the cells and contributes to scent as well.

As mentioned earlier, larger breeds of dogs have at least 200 million olfactory cells used to detect scent. Even the smaller breeds of dogs have at least 125 million olfactory cells.

The nasal cavity of dogs is also 4 times the size of the nasal cavity of humans, giving them a larger area in which scent is held and processed. In addition, dogs' mouths act as receptors for scent.

The scent article is a key item in a search mission, and can be any item that was worn or used and last touched by the lost person. The scent article is used so trailing dogs and some air scent dogs can identify the scent of the missing person that they must find.

Scientists are beginning to understand the role of the *vomeronasal organ,* a pair of sacs located above the roof of the mouth just behind the incisors that open by ducts into both the nose and mouth. Put simply, it's believed that the vomeronasal organ, is an accessory olfactory organ that enables animals to not only identify scent in the form of skin rafts and surrounding vapors, but quite possibly to identify the chemical and/or hormonal composition of scent in all its complexity. This may explain how dogs know when a person is anxious or afraid, or when someone's been injured. Research and training are also under way using dogs to detect cancer cells in people. Research is showing that dogs can identify the presence of cancer in people where technology has failed to detect it; many of these people had been diagnosed as cancer-free using current technology, before the dog identified the presence of cancer. In addition to cancer detection, dogs are being trained to alert their owners to pending epileptic seizures. The changes in hormonal and chemical balance in the body, respiration, or cells may be what the dogs are detecting.

Another excellent resource for information on dogs' scenting ability, as well as the nature and behavior of scent, can be found in the book, *Scent and the Scenting Dog* by William G. Syrotuck (Barkleigh Productions, 1972).

Scent Value

Understanding the nature of scent is only the first step in understanding what's happening for the search dog. The next step is to realize the variations in what the dog will encounter

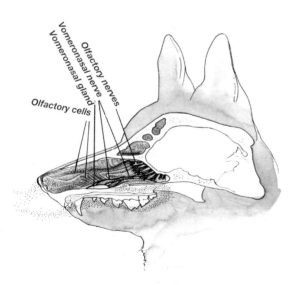

A dog's physiology enables it to detect minute particles of scent. The olfactory nerve cells connect to the temporal lobes of the brain where memory is stored.

Moist, humid climates encourage the growth of bacteria and enhance scent.

when working scent. Scent is dynamic, due to many natural and man-made influences. Search dog handlers need to recognize these dynamics so they can interpret each situation and be an effective partner to their dog by supporting their scenting abilities.

As rafts are sloughed off, they may immediately stick to surfaces or blow around an area before settling on a surface. As the rafts settle, they mix with humidity, which encourages the growth of bacteria and enhances the quality of the scent. Dogs respond more dramatically to scent in moist, shaded areas because the moisture increases the longevity and the strength of the scent. Contrary to popular misconception, water does not immediately wash away or eliminate scent. Although a heavy, prolonged downpour may wash scent

away, water can and does freshen scent. Dog handlers often notice areas where their dogs get stuck on a search in the wilderness because the scent is so pervasive or strong. An example might be a damp, marshy area. The moisture encourages the growth of the bacteria and strengthens the quality of the scent in the marsh, even though the missing person may have moved quickly through it. The reason dogs have a hard time moving out of these areas is that the scent in the dampness stays fresh longer than the scent in the drier surrounding area.

Skin rafts remain viable even in bodies of water, such as lakes. Again, the cells absorb the moisture and move with the water currents. Eventually the scent rises to the surface, where it may be moved again by the air currents, possibly settling in vegetation or catching against an embankment. Water search dogs have been able to identify victims of drowning who are more than 30 feet below the surface of the water. Since snow is frozen water, its effects on scent are similar. In fact, when there's no chance that an avalanche victim has survived, the avalanche dog handler may wait to search the debris field until the scent of the victim has had time to percolate to the surface of the snow.

Moving water, like wind, keeps the skin rafts flowing and affects the behavior of scent. Searches along riverbanks have shown that scent moves downstream quickly, reflecting the speed of the water. Tests have been done using dye to simulate the effects moving water has on the movement of scent. At the point where the dye was deposited, a minimal amount floated up to the surface of the water. However, a greater quantity of dye rose to the surface one mile downstream, and more still rose another mile downstream—two miles from the original point of entry! During water searches, dogs often literally bite the water (not the same as drinking the water) to identify the scent.

Whereas humidity and moisture enhance the effectiveness of scent, the lack of humidity contributes to the skin rafts drying out, which decreases the quality of the scent. Wind also has a drying effect on skin rafts, just as it dries out the body's skin. Dryness causes rapid dehydration of the rafts, minimizing the growth of bacteria and making it more difficult to hold the scent for very long. Trailing dog handlers in the arid southwestern United States have watched their dogs struggle with ground scent on hot summer days, only to see the same dog easily work the same scent six hours later in relatively cool evening temperatures. This is not to say that it's impossible to work a trailing dog in a dry climate, just that it presents different problems for the remarkable scent detection abilities of the dog.

In fact, a dog that's trained to search in an arid climate usually has difficulty transitioning to a humid climate where the ground is covered with more vegetation. One reason for this appears to be that the dog learns to compensate for the weaker scent on the dry terrain in an arid climate. Greater moisture content and denser vegetation means more intense scent from all sources (including wildlife) for the search dog, which may be overwhelming at first. It's as if there is too much scent to follow in any one direction. The dog handler must be aware of these variations to provide support so the dog can work most effectively. In this case, the support a handler provides for their search dog is to offer plenty of water because it's important to keep a search dog hydrated under normal conditions. Drier conditions require water at more frequent intervals. Not only does this re-hydrate the dog, but it also moistens the mouth and nasal membranes, improving the dog's ability to detect and follow the scent to its source.

Some trailing dog handlers may also wet their dogs' noses at regular intervals to help re-hydrate the membranes of the nasal passages.

How Scent Behaves

Although dogs have the perfect physiology for detecting scent, in order to place the dogs correctly, handlers need to know how to visualize scent as well. Where the search dog detects and follows scent, the dog's handler needs to be able to put the dog in the best position possible to find the scent. To do this, handlers must understand or *read* what is happening to the scent they're asking the dog to find.

While moisture affects the quality of scent, terrain can affect how the scent behaves and therefore how the dog is able to work with the scent. For example, drainages and depressions frequently hold scent. Because drainages or gullies are often shaded and cooler than the surrounding higher ground, scent frequently stays in low drainages longer, causing the dog to stay in the drainages with the stronger scent. When this happens, the handler may need to lead the dog out of the drainage to enable the dog to determine whether scent is even present above the drainage or only found in the low area. It's likely the handler won't know whether this is the case until the dog moves into a position to be able to make that determination.

Arid climates minimize the growth of bacteria, causing scent to dry out faster than it would under more humid conditions.

In the Rocky Mountains, scent also catches between rocks and in cracks among boulders. Although rocks are obviously hard and usually dry, they provide the shaded cracks, crevices, and depressions where scent can settle and be held as if in a pocket. Search dogs in the Rocky Mountain region often climb large rock outcroppings and sniff these cracks, even though the person may never have climbed the rocks, but instead walked around the base. The scent that's been blown into these crevices is simply stronger than it is on the ground. The dogs eventually continue to search the area around and beyond the boulders once they eliminate the boulders as the source of the scent.

It's easy to imagine the influence of wind on extremely tiny skin rafts.

It is important to keep search dogs hydrated and their noses moist.

Search dog handlers often carry flagging tape or puff bottles containing powder to assist in visualizing the current direction of the wind. By watching how the flagging tape is blown by the wind or the direction in which the powder blows, handlers' awareness of the effect the wind might have on the scent the dogs are working is far greater than if they simply felt the wind on their skin or in their hair. A dog may become aware of the scent from a person who is more than a mile away if the wind is blowing fairly hard in open terrain. As long as the wind is blowing steadily from the same direction, the dog can move quickly to locate the person.

But, what if the wind shifts direction or dies? Air scent dog handlers need to be able to move their dogs into the wind to enable them to relocate the rafts. Shifting winds can also work to the handlers' advantage by giving them enough information to triangulate on an area where the scent appears to originate. To do this, they use a map and compass to chart the dog's *alert* to the scent on a map, along with the wind direction at the time of the alert. As they review the dog's alert, handlers begin to see where the subject is or was at the time of the dog's alerts. The advantage of deploying several air scent dogs on a mission is that they can confirm one another's information, which can then be triangulated on a map. When charting wind direction and alerts from dogs in multiple locations, it's possible to pinpoint where the scent source is likely to be located, like pieces of a puzzle that drop into place.

Temperature can also affect the behavior of scent. Heat rises, and on warm, sunny slopes, scent also rises. Scent actually rises or travels *up slope* in the warmth of the morning sun as ridge tops are heated. An air scent dog handler will place the dog on a ridge top in the morning in an attempt to determine if the person is below the ridge. In the cool of the evening, lower temperatures cause scent to descend or move *down slope.* So the same air scent team would work the valley bottom late in the day, hoping to locate a person walking along the top of the ridge.

Even when temperatures are below freezing, the warmth of the sun causes scent to rise, even beneath layers of snow.

High temperatures can also bake the skin rafts and dry them out so that the scent is more difficult, perhaps even impossible to detect. Many people are under the impression that dogs who follow ground scent work with their noses very close to the ground at all times. However, since heat causes scent to rise, it may no longer be viable on the hot, dry ground. Trailing dogs are frequently seen working with their heads higher on dry summer days because the scent has risen. It can actually be stronger anywhere from 6 to 18 inches above the ground. It's not unusual to see a trailing dog working slowly in the summer, with its head held higher in a hot, open area with minimal vegetation, then work quickly, with its nose close to the ground when it moves into the cooler, shaded, wooded areas on the same search.

At the other extreme, frigid temperatures can cause scent to diminish and lay dormant (frozen) in a very small area. The frozen rafts and small scent area could make it necessary for the dog to be almost on top of the scent source before being able to pinpoint the location of the person. An example of this was a search for a person following a sudden snowstorm in March, where the wind chill was at least –20°F at the time of the search and the snow in the area was extremely cold. All five search dog

✦ **SEARCH BRIEF** ✦

A search dog's *alert* is the behavior it has been trained to display when it finds the target scent. An alert is critical information because it means that the dog has found the scent for which it has been searching.

teams reported that the dogs indicated the subject's scent was emanating from the same area. The dogs showed no interest when they approached the area that had been identified as most likely, and were drawn to an adjoining area by scent in the air. When discussing the dogs' findings with the sheriff, the handlers were able to consider the effects of the frigid temperatures and help identify the most likely target location. The subject was later discovered buried beneath the snow in the area of initial interest. It seemed his scent had traveled below the snow's surface through the vents created by crevices between surrounding boulders, only to escape some distance away into the sunny area where the ground and air were warmer. No scent seemed to be rising in what was later found to be an area of about 50 yards immediately surrounding the person. Due to the dangerous conditions and terrain, no dogs were able to get directly over the body.

Another influence on the behavior of scent is the age of the scent. As skin rafts age and dry out, their

Contamination is considered to be any type or amount of scent that could interfere with a search dog's ability to identify the target scent.

potency appears to diminish. As described earlier, humidity and the moisture content of cells aid in the growth of bacteria on the rafts, so scent stays "fresh" longer in the presence of humidity. Residual scent can stay viable for several days in more humid conditions. In arid climates, scent can become indistinguishable in less than 48 hours in the summer. A trailing dog handler needs to know the approximate age of the residual scent to know the likelihood of the dog's ability to fol-

Flagging tape helps search dog handlers monitor the velocity and direction of wind.

low through. Scent can refresh over time, as well. The previously dried-out skin rafts may also become re-hydrated after a cool period in which moisture is added back into the cells. The handler needs to be able to weigh the likelihood of this happening, along with the age of the scent, when responding with a trailing dog. Although the age of the skin rafts affects the quality of residual scent, it's important to note that age does not seem to diminish the scent coming directly from a person. In fact, dogs can detect scent directly from a source years after a body has deteriorated and only bones remain, or even when the only scent remaining is what's left in the soil.

Contamination is another factor to consider when reading scent. All search areas are subject to influences from other scent sources, but some types and amounts of contamination can affect a dog's work more than others. Exhaust fumes could potentially overwhelm a dog's ability to pinpoint scent. Exhaust from snowmobiles and all-terrain vehicles (A.T.V.s) are difficult to work around, as are trucks and cars when the engines are running. Search dogs are often transported on snowmobiles and A.T.V.s to the search area, but it's important to then turn the vehicles off or clear the vehicles completely out of the search area as quickly as possible. Because vehicles left idling in a search area can obliterate any trace of residual scent, handlers will often ask the mission leader or sheriff to let them start working their dogs before vehicles arrive in the search area, when possible.

Another type of contamination is the scent left by others. Scent discrimination requires that search dogs distinguish the specific scent of the missing individual (*scent discriminate*). However, even when the dog is focused on the individual's scent, a large amount of scent from other sources can influence how quickly or how well a dog can work. More distinct scents also mean more scent for a search dog to eliminate while attempting to discover and follow the scent of a particular person. This added complication may add time to the dog's progress, simply because of the time it takes to work carefully through the variety of scent influences. For this reason, search dog handlers prefer to have their dogs begin searching before too many other people move into the area. When possible, this option can save valuable time for dog teams on a search, because they can work quickly with less contamination.

Even search dogs that are not trained to discriminate between the scents of individual humans are trained to ignore the scent of animals during a search. Dogs have an amazing ability to eliminate extraneous scents, so it's difficult to say exactly how much natural contamination is too much. The amount a dog is able to effectively search through seems to depend on the individual dog, and must be considered on each mission.

Other factors influencing the methods search dogs use to follow

When temperatures rise and the ground warms up, trailing dogs work with their noses higher to follow residual scent.

scent have to do with where the scent is found. The dynamic behavior of scent described so far affects both scent on the ground and scent in the air. The manner in which both trailing dogs and air scent dogs work with scent is also affected by these influences.

Ground Scent

When skin rafts are sloughed off the body, some float to the ground and some are blown by the wind away from their original source. Of those that are blown by the wind, many land among vegetation and rocks or anything that could contain them close to the ground. This type of scent is referred to as *ground scent.* The fact that the source is no longer in the location of the existing scent is what classifies it as residual scent. In other words, it's what remains after the source has left. Residual scent is also left on objects

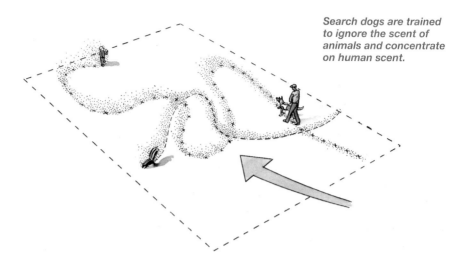

Search dogs are trained to ignore the scent of animals and concentrate on human scent.

or articles that have been touched or worn by a person, even after that person has discarded the article and left the area.

Bacteria, from body secretions such as perspiration, remain viable as the skin cells fall from the body. These

A trailing dog follows scent that has fallen to the ground.

bacteria enshroud the raft in vapor and continue to grow and multiply. As they grow, they maintain the unique identity of their source—the person from whom the rafts were shed. If moisture mixes with the rafts after they land on the ground, the bacteria grow, maintaining the integrity of what humans interpret as scent. Trailing dogs find and follow the scent on the ground, wherever it settles. When scent is blown by the wind, it needs to be caught by some feature to be considered ground scent.

Not so surprisingly then, ground scent is often found by trailing dogs many yards away from where the person actually traveled. The distance scent travels is based on the velocity of the wind. Trailing dogs have been observed trailing scent several feet from the actual path taken by the person they're trailing. In fact, the scent from rafts that have blown some distance from the path of travel may be more intense than that from rafts that land along the exact route. This is because the density of the rafts and bacteria is greater at their final destination than at their point of origin. The reason for this has less to do with how far the scent travels than what happens to the rafts at their final destination.

When some feature on the land catches the rafts, the viability of the bacteria is determined by the quality of the environment. If they land in an area that's protected from the heat and drying effects of the sun, there's a definite likelihood that the scent will remain strong for some time. Mentioned earlier was the interest that trailing dogs often show in scent that is caught in the cracks and crevices of rock outcroppings and boulders. Although the surface is hard, the shaded crevices act as pockets that collect and hold scent in a small space, as well as provide a cooler temperature for the bacteria to grow. These crevices often hold moisture too, which further encourages the growth of bacteria, thereby intensifying the scent.

Search dogs are often seen sniffing under logs, around bushes, trees, and grassy areas. Scent that is caught in vegetation may not always stay low. The rafts also get caught in the branches of bushes, where the scent is detected higher up. On summer days the ground temperature can be much hotter than the temperature in the air. For this reason, scent that gets caught in the leafy branches of vegetation and held in the shade stays viable longer. It's always impressive to

Scent may blow from its original source and settle under tree limbs, rocks, and vegetation.

see a trailing dog, sophisticated in scenting techniques, sniff the very tip of a blade of grass to determine where a person moved. No doubt, the person left his signature scent on the blade of grass when he brushed it with his leg as he walked by.

Although it's true that obstacles catch and contain scent, scent also follows the path of least resistance, such as roads, cleared paths, and drainages. The clearings can act as channels for the scent as it's carried with the prevailing winds. These areas may create problems for a trailing dog because the scent is carried along the cleared area, even when the person merely crosses the road or drainage.

As time passes, ground scent matures, intensifies, and then deteriorates. As the rafts dry out, bacteria dies and the scent loses its integrity.

Scent follows channels created by pathways and roads, and collects in rock crevices; a trailing dog must determine the location of the strongest scent to find its source.

Within the first four hours of being deposited, skin rafts may still blow around an area and, although the scent is fresher, it may not have completely settled. The actual scent often begins to intensify after the rafts settle in an environment hospitable to the growth of bacteria. Ground scent that has settled and aged for more than four hours may be easier for a trailing dog to follow. Up to a point, the scent continues to intensify. Then, as the scent continues to age, its intensity wanes and becomes markedly diminished. The length of time scent remains viable is again influenced by the environmental factors of the area in which the rafts are deposited. In hot, arid climates scent may be undetectable after eight hours, whereas scent in a cooler, more moist climate can maintain its integrity for days because moisture helps replenish bacteria. As the bacteria age and die and the quality of

scent deteriorates, more mature trailing dogs are still able to detect and follow the weaker or more limited particles of scent. However, at some point in time the skin rafts become completely dehydrated and even the most experienced trailing dog can no longer detect the aged, residual scent.

Air Scent

Skin rafts that are sloughed off the body and remain in the air are blown by a breeze or wind and may even be blown a great distance. The skin rafts that are carried in the air appear to form a sort of cone, or *scent cone,* that expands as the rafts move farther away from their source. Scent carried in the air is referred to as *air scent.* The key characteristics of air scent are that it travels through the air instead of settling on the ground, and that it emanates directly from the source at its current location. As scent that has been carried in the air settles on the ground, it becomes ground scent. Ground scent may become airborne again, as well. Air scent dogs look for and detect scent that emanates directly from a person or article as it's carried in the air.

Scent that is detected at scenes of disaster, from beneath water, or through snow in avalanche debris fields is being carried in the air, although it's filtering around concrete rubble, through water, or snow. In these situations, the tragedy occurred in the past, but as long as the missing person is at the scene, skin cells are being sloughed off, bacteria are growing, vapor is forming, and their scent is present in the air. The scenting technique used by search dogs on these types of missions is air scent.

The quality of scent emanating from a person remains high because skin cells are continually being sloughed off, replenishing those that have blown away or are otherwise destroyed. As the rafts are blown farther away from their source, they're more widely dispersed. For this reason, the effect wind has on the integrity of air scent is dramatic. The speed and velocity of the wind determines how far rafts blow and how quickly they're dispersed. The direction of the wind is also a factor for air scent dogs because they must constantly work into the wind in order to locate the scent as it's carried from its source.

Assuming the direction, speed, and velocity of the wind remain constant (which is rare), the direction in which the lost person travels affects where the air scent dog is able to find scent in relation to where the dog is searching. For example, if the air scent dog team has detected a person while moving directly into the wind, their ability to get to the person may depend on where the person moves as the dog approaches. If the person changes direction, she may eventually move out of the direct line of scent for the dog. When this happens, the handler ultimately needs to be able to move the dog back into a position that is in line with the person, based on where scent is most

+ **SEARCH BRIEF** +

Skin rafts and their surrounding vapors that are carried in the air get caught in vegetation, trees, and other obstacles. Air scent dogs also recognize scent when it's settled, but because it's residual scent and not emanating directly from its source, they may acknowledge it through a passive indication rather than an alert, and should always continue to look for the fresher scent from the source.

likely to be found. The handler must do this without knowing if or where the person is moving. In this situation, the wind direction remains constant, but the lost person shifts her direction, causing the scent cone to shift as well.

The movement of skin rafts is also affected by the flow of currents under debris, in snow, and in the water. The

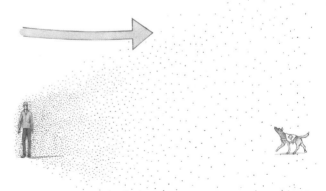

Air borne scent expands from the source in a cone shape or scent cone. Air scent dogs follow the scent cone to its source.

Noting the wind direction, a water search dog handler watches as her dog reacts to scent in the lake.

Avalanche dog handlers consider these dynamics and understand their dogs' alerts are often downwind from the actual burial. Water currents also move scent before it rises to the surface. Even when a lake looks still, currents continue to flow beneath the surface, and determine how far from the source scent rises before it reaches the air and is picked up by the wind. The effect of flowing water is much more dramatic due to the speed and force with which the water travels. The experiment mentioned earlier, where dye was dropped into a stream, shows that the scent of a body in moving water may travel several miles downstream from the original location before rising to the surface, where it can be detected by a search dog.

The direction in which the air scent dog team moves is critical, because their path and pattern of travel determine whether or not they can locate a person's scent. As mentioned earlier, it's highly likely that a dog could pick up the scent of someone who's a mile away, yet, if it's a hot, dry day and the wind is also dry, the skin rafts and their surrounding vapors from bacteria could dry up within a half of a mile from the missing person. It's also possible that an experienced air scent dog could walk by a person and not locate him if the wind is blowing his scent away from the dog. Air scent dog handlers learn to guide their dogs so they can use the changeable nature of wind to their dog's advantage.

scent is dynamic in that it's being carried by the flow of air or water and is constantly replenished as more cells and oil from the skin are discarded. In rubble piles, the scent is channeled by the flow of air as it travels down or up shafts or under and around blocks of concrete before it rises to the surface. For this reason, the location where a search dog detects a person buried in rubble may be some distance away from the person. The same is true for dogs that pick up the scent of people buried under snow. Because snow is porous, air carries scent under the layers of snow even when the snow is packed as hard as concrete, as it is following most avalanches. Then, once the scent rises in the avalanche debris field, it's carried by the air currents among and around the blocks of snow and in the air above the surface of the snow.

Chapter Five
Training Basics

People familiar with dogs and curious about search dogs sometimes wonder why formal training is required, since dogs have an innate ability to detect scent. Training establishes the basis for learning the technical skills needed to meet the demands of search and rescue. A well-developed training program addresses the individual needs of each dog and handler and ultimately contributes to the development of both, enabling them to become an effective team.

Beginning exercises establish the foundation upon which all other exercises are built. The ultimate objective of search dog training is to teach the dog to look for someone in response to a command, while working in partnership with his or her handler. A search dog is also trained to consistently communicate the location of the scent source to its handler. This trained indication may involve taking the handler to the victim, digging in snow, lying down over a burial site, barking at a disaster site, or other possibilities.

Training and practice should always be fun for a search dog team, and each exercise needs to be set up so that the dog can be successful. Even when the handler provides assistance to the dog, it should be a positive experience in which both partners learn more about their team's capabilities.

Training Objectives for the Dog

Training provides the focus required for most of the work dogs accomplish for people. Dogs that work stock are a good example. Although dogs bred for herding are born with the instinct to move livestock, this ability alone is not enough to achieve the goals envisioned by the sheepherder. To do this, coordination between the dog and the handler is necessary. Training provides the means by which a dog's innate abilities are channeled to accomplish a specific job. In fact, training hones the dog's skills to the level of expertise required by the conditions of the job.

In search and rescue, a dog's natural ability to detect scent is refined so that the dog can discover a scent, follow it, and find the source of a particular scent. In addition, however, the dog must be able to communicate the information to the handler who, in turn, must be able to understand the information.

Once a dog learns to search for people on command, it can be trained to stay focused on a single scent while ignoring the many other scents constantly mingling together. The ability to distinguish between multiple scents, or *scent discrimination,* is extremely valuable for a search dog and most search dogs can learn this skill fairly quickly. Through training, it's possible to guide the dog to a level of experience where it is able to ignore or work through conflicting scent and follow only the unique scent of the lost person.

Scent discrimination is required for trailing dogs, and it's also a valuable tool for dogs using air-scenting tech-

A wilderness search dog clearly indicates the victim's pack on a search.

niques, although it's not mandatory in every situation. Whereas trailing dogs need to know which scent on the ground they're being asked to follow, air scent dogs have the option to locate any person currently in their search area. However, even dogs using air scenting techniques at the scene of a disaster or an avalanche, where locating anyone in the defined area is the goal, may be trained to prioritize the scent of a live person over the scent of a body or buried articles.

While training a dog to discriminate between the scents of individuals, a search dog is also trained to locate and identify clues that may lead to the particular person for whom they're searching. In this valuable tool in wilderness search, the dog clearly indicates articles (which are clues) dropped by the missing person. In the process, the dog ignores all other objects that are not associated with the missing person. To accomplish this, the dog is trained to clearly identify the clue to the handler through a trained indication or a specific signal such as barking, lying down, pawing, or retrieving the article. The ability to locate clues is valuable in vast areas where the incident commander needs to determine where to send other dog teams, searchers, or helicopters. One clue can change the course and, ultimately, the outcome of a search. Dogs used for forensic evidence are trained to locate decomposed human tissue or body fluids that remain in the soil, on an article, or in a building. Their ability to precisely identify this evidence may contribute to the investigation of a crime, and for this reason, they must be accurate.

Throughout training, the dog and handler develop a sense of partnership. The dog learns the requirements of its handler as well as the manner in which they must work. Some beginning handlers comment that their dogs possibly could accomplish what's required without a handler. Although it's true that the dog may be able to follow its nose for simple problems, a search dog needs a handler who understands the situation, can provide guidance, develops a strategy or plan for the search, and responds effectively to the situation at hand. Training scenarios create situations and experiences that build the type of partnership where a dog and handler know what to expect from one another.

Training Objectives for the Handler

One of the jobs of search dog handlers is to enable their dog to work according to its natural capabilities. Whether the handler can determine how the dog works best is directly related to the manner in which the dog is trained. Positive reinforcement is the most effective type of motivation for a search dog. Positive reinforcement is used when

┌─────────────────────────────────┐
│   ✣ **SEARCH BRIEF** ✣   │
│   │
│ Training objectives for the dog: │
│ • to find and follow scent   │
│ • to discriminate among multiple │
│   scents   │
│ • to locate clues   │
│ • to work in partnership with the │
│   handler.   │
└─────────────────────────────────┘

the handler guides the dog and encourages the desired behavior instead of forcing a behavior by using a negative correction.

The alternative is when handlers provide answers for their dog and fail to either strengthen the dog's natural abilities or to learn how their dog solves problems. In search and rescue, a problem may simply be a new situation or one that presents a challenge to the dog. Observing how the dog works with problems teaches the handler how the dog thinks through various situations and where the dog needs guidance.

Positive reinforcement emphasizes the dog's ability to find solutions that may ultimately determine the direction of the search. While handlers encourage the dog to follow the correct scent, they are also learning to assess each situation so they can assist the dog if it becomes necessary. When the dog is confused or faces a challenge that it is unable to resolve by itself, handlers can then use either the lead or their voice to gently guide the dog into a position where the dog can complete the exercise successfully.

A handler discusses strategy with mission base.

Another objective for handlers is to learn, develop, and implement effective search strategies. Strategies used by search dog handlers are those aimed at assisting their search dogs to achieve their goals by placing them in positions where they have the greatest potential to succeed. To do this, the handlers must be able to assess each situation. Once they become comfortable with their dog's abilities, the handlers can develop and follow various strategies and make adjustments to help their dogs. One example of a search strategy is when the handler assesses several factors in a search and determines how the dog can work to its greatest advantage. Considerations might include the most likely area in which the victim will be found, the effect of wind and weather on the scent, terrain features, and any dangers associated with a particular search. Any of these considerations may determine the best placement of dog teams, the best access routes into and out of an area, and the search disciplines to be used.

Strategy doesn't end when the dog teams return to mission base. As dog handlers are debriefed by the incident commander, they describe what the dogs showed them through their alerts or negative indications and what this meant to the handlers, as they review maps of the search area. They are often asked to use this information to assess the best area in which to place additional resources, such as foot teams (searchers without dogs), planes, or helicopters, and/or the most probable area in which the missing subject will be found.

✤ SEARCH BRIEF ✤

A *negative indication* is when the search dog determines where the victim *is not located or did not travel.* For example, in an exercise for a trailing dog, when the dog turns left and away from a body of water, the handler could consider this a *negative indication* because the scent did not turn right toward the lake.

Building Confidence

The whole training experience should be a positive one for both the dog and the handler, because the positive nature of training increases the likelihood that the team members will continue to work well together. As the dog and the handler's capabilities expand, they gain confidence in each other and are able to face new and more complex challenges.

Each training exercise is created to address a specific problem or set of challenges, such as turns or contaminated scent. Confidence is developed when the dog team works hard, yet feels good about their accomplishments.

Conversely, both the dog and the handler become frustrated when they feel as if they've failed, even though the particular training scenario may be more complex than the last. Therefore, it's good to simplify the scope covered by each initial training scenario when adding a new challenge.

For example, when adding turns to a pattern for a trailing dog, it's helpful to shorten the distance of the trail and/or lessen the time the scent ages, even though the dog has previously worked over long distances on straight trails where the scent aged for a longer period of time. In this way, the dog can concentrate on working out the new problem of turns. Another example of a way in which the scope of a problem can be simplified is when an air scent dog, previously trained to find cadaver scent or decomposed tissue in a moderately large area above ground, is first exposed to tissue that is buried. In this situation, it's good to limit the size of the area to be searched so that the dog can spend its time and energy working through the challenges created by the buried tissue and its scent mixing with the soil.

Confidence from fellow team members is also valuable. The best search situations are ones where multiple dog teams are deployed. Multiple teams can corroborate and follow through with search strategies based on one another's information. For this reason, it's helpful for dog teams to be familiar with how each works, as well as each team's effectiveness under the particular conditions. The best way to achieve this shared confidence is by training together. Handlers often accompany each other during training exercises to observe and offer advice. In this way, they become acquainted with one another's style and gain confidence in the quality of their work on actual search missions.

Confidence from searchers who do not work dogs is also beneficial. When dog handlers report their find-

---

⊹ SEARCH BRIEF ⊹

Objectives for the handler:
- to learn how the dog works
- to encourage the dog, to guide the dog
- to develop search strategy skills

---

ings over the radio or directly to a mission leader, other searchers as well as people at mission base evaluate the information. The handler's confidence in his or her own dog is transmitted along with the information. Incident commanders, mission leaders, and other searchers familiar with the quality of the dog team's capabilities may rely more heavily on their information when they hear the handler's own confidence. Search personnel who aren't dog handlers often benefit from training with search dog teams, because they also gain a better understanding of the value of dogs as a resource.

A search dog tells his handler he's found the victim. Training for a search dog is based on positive learning experiences, rewards, and mutual confidence.

This confidence in the dogs' abilities was displayed many times over following the collapse of the World Trade Center in New York City. A disaster response dog handler (qualified as a canine search specialist with FEMA's Urban Task Force) and her dog were returning to their base of operations after working a 12-hour shift. Several firefighters had been digging and removing rubble for two hours to get down to where they believed a victim's body was located in an area that was separate from the dog team's assigned search area. The firefighters asked the dog handler for help from her dog in defining the correct direction to dig. She and her dog worked the area and, although the dog was trained to find live victims, the dog was able to determine the most concentrated area of scent in moments. The handler said, "My dog says you should be digging over here," which is where the body was found.

Reading the Dog

Handlers must first learn to be sensitive to their dog in order to accurately interpret information communicated by the dog. A good training program provides opportunities for handlers to understand their dog's strengths as well as its limitations. *Reading the dog* is a term used to describe how well handlers interpret the dog's behavior. In reading the dog, handlers learn to watch the dog work and translate what they

The best way to learn is to train with other dog handlers.

believe is happening, based on their experience under similar circumstances. Accuracy becomes important when the handler translates the dog's findings for other individuals. Dog handlers rely on their own understanding of their dog to communicate effectively with the dog, other team members, and incident commanders or mission coordinators. A particularly sensitive handler may even be able to determine the condition or movement of the missing person by interpreting the dog's behavior. Examples of this are handlers who are able to determine whether the missing person is running away, sitting in one place, or even dead, based on their dog's demeanor.

The best way to learn to read a search dog is to watch the dog work through the challenges presented in training. Of course, this must be accomplished in a controlled situation where the handler knows the

Recognizing a dog's facial expressions is an important aspect of learning to read a search dog.

nature of the problem. Advanced training offers opportunities to set up problems without the handler's previous knowledge of the scenario. Once the problem is completed, the handler can then review each stage of the scenario with those who are aware of the challenges. Follow-up discussion assists the handler in understanding what the dog found and, most likely, communicated to the handler at each stage.

Learning to read the dog is another reason handlers try to discover the dog's style of working rather than impose their own preconceived assumptions on the dog. With the emphasis on discovery, handlers can answer many of the questions that typically arise. How does the dog behave when it's looking for scent, has found the scent, or has lost the scent? Is the dog actively working the scent? Is the dog following an animal? Has the dog determined that there is no scent in the area or that scent did exist but has completely disappeared? If so, at what point was the dog still actively working the scent? If the handler never allows the dog to work out problems using the dog's own strengths, the handler won't be able to answer these questions when they arise during actual missions.

Assisting the Dog

There are times when handlers are required to help their dogs. It's important to remember that the handler is the other half of the dog team and is expected to be able help the dog during the search. A search dog needs to expend its energy searching rather than figuring out confusing situations alone. By learning to read the dog, the handler is able to understand when the dog is having problems with a situation during a search. It's frequently appropriate for handlers to help their dog when they recognize that the dog is unable to solve a problem alone, thus minimizing pressure on the dog and saving valuable time. Assisting the dog may be as simple as taking the dog back to a location where it appeared to be working well with the scent.

The first step in helping the search dog is to recognize when assistance is necessary. A simple example is where access to an area is physically obstructed. The dog may work frantically to follow the scent but be unable to overcome an obstacle. In this example, the handler recognizes the problem and leads the dog along the safest route. Using the example described, the dog's frantic behavior as it tries to get through the obstacle is the clue that the handler should help. Training provides the experience necessary to understand when the dog needs help, because cues from the dog are not always straightforward. It also teaches the dog to let the handler know when it needs help.

Some dogs whine when they can't resolve a problem and, in this case, are sending auditory signals that assistance is needed. However, some difficulties that arise may not

be as apparent to the handler. Many dogs will continue to try to resolve a scent problem by themselves while they expend energy and time. These dogs may become frustrated and even lose precious motivation in the attempt. At some point, handlers should be able to see that the dog is having difficulty and intercede. They should be able to determine where the dog began having problems with the scent and take the dog to a location where the problem can be resolved more easily.

Knowing How to Help the Dog

The key word for the type of assistance a search dog may need is *guidance*. When the dog needs help to get through a problem, it's better to lead or guide the dog into an area where the dog can solve the problem. Without transferring frustration through their voice, handlers can calmly say, "Let's go over here" and take the dog to the area where they believe the problem can be resolved. In the case of a trailing dog, handlers must take the dog back to the location where they believe the dog worked effectively before becoming confused or losing the scent. This gives the dog another opportunity to work out the problem and determine the direction of the most concentrated residual scent. An air scent problem often requires that the handler move the dog into another area or to a different elevation where the wind is more likely to blow scent to the dog.

Whether trailing or air scenting, the search dog should always walk in front of the handler while moving out of and into an area, as if the dog were leading. By leading, the dog is in a position to take control along the way if or when it finds the scent or

A search dog sits in front of his handler as a signal he needs some assistance.

rediscovers the lost scent. Keeping the dog in front also enables the handler to continue to observe the dog.

Always Winning

A search dog's motivation to work is valuable and should be encouraged. Through encouragement, the dog always feels as if it contributes to the resolution of the problem and can begin to search again, often without further assistance from the handler. Placing the dog in situations where it is most likely to succeed contributes to the dog's motivation. Although this is not always possible in actual search situations, it is possible when training in a controlled setting. When the exercises are designed in such a way that the dog achieves the objective, training can be both challenging and rewarding. Conversely, merely setting the dog up to fail in order to discover the dog's limits during training leaves everyone feeling frustrated. Some dogs simply quit working when they become too frustrated and when they're either prevented from or unable to resolve a problem.

Finding the balance between encouraging the dog to work out challenging situations on its own, providing assistance when needed, and taking over for the dog is not always easy. Helping the dog is not the same as taking over the dog's job, which should be avoided at all times. No human can do what a trained search dog is able to do.

Using praise and encouragement to help the dog accomplish its job keeps the dog in charge of resolving the confusing situation.

Training Sites

The training environment was mentioned briefly in Chapter 3. Training sites and scenarios should correspond as much as possible to the geography and situations in which the dog will actually work. People rarely get lost in city parks or while hiking on marked trails. Therefore, when training to find people lost in the wilderness, the majority of training takes place off of well-traveled paths. When training a dog for avalanche rescue, it's necessary to work where the snow is deep and consistent with the type of snow that's most likely to collapse or avalanche in the region. Disaster response dogs must train in sites that mimic the challenges of collapsed structures and the chaotic conditions following a disaster. They also must be trained to navigate the numerous situations they'll encounter using an obstacle course, with dynamic opportunities where problems vary frequently. Training at sites that mimic actual search areas and situations help prepare the dog team for the real situations they will encounter on a search.

The Work Area

The size and geography of areas used when training a search dog

Without understanding the dynamics of scent, an air scent dog handler cannot place his dog where it's most likely to find scent.

should be appropriate for the level of training the dog is receiving. A dog just beginning search training works in areas that are relatively small. Beginning exercises are designed to introduce the dog and handler to scent work. Problems are created specifically so that the dog team can reach each goal quickly over a short distance.

The size requirements of the training area expand fairly quickly. As the novice dog team becomes more experienced, they are able to cover more terrain than during the early stages of training. The dog team also becomes able to work on more difficult problems.

The size of the area is determined by the complexity of the problem that has been set up for the dog and handler, as well as the sophistication of the team. Adding turns to a trailing

A search dog handler must be able to guide the dog to a location where a high probability of finding a victim's scent exists—if the victim is in the area.

exercise requires a larger area than one where the dog is expected to move in a single direction. Advanced air scent problems are set up in areas large enough to require the dog to search for some time before locating the subject.

As training progresses, problems become more complex and the setting also increases in complexity. When training a dog for water search, training progresses steadily from simple problems in shallow, still water. More advanced problems are set up in larger bodies of deeper water or rapidly flowing water where the scent is influenced by thermodynamics and movement.

Topography and Terrain Features

Novice exercises are set up in fields or open meadows away from buildings and heavy ground cover. The terrain should be relatively flat and open, to enable the handler to work close enough to see each movement the dog makes. At least in the early stages of training, the handler should be no more than 30 feet from the dog while working. Another advantage of flat, open space is that the focus of the exercise is on teaching the dog to use its nose to locate people, rather than on figuring out the complex behavior of scent under various terrain conditions. As the exercises increase in difficulty for the novice dog, the handler becomes more adept at watching, reading, and guiding the dog through turns, scent contamination and other challenges in open areas, preparing it for the next level of training—which incorporates the influences of terrain on scent.

Topography creates a new set of training challenges because of the way scent moves. Once a trailing dog masters turns or an air scent dog becomes proficient in more level open areas, it can begin to work among diverse terrain features. Terrain features can include hills, mountains, meadows, forests, streams, lakes, buildings, and roads. The behavior of scent was discussed in more detail in the previous chapter. Here it's important to understand that the type of terrain features that are typical of a team's search area must be incorporated into training. When training is designed using the features the team will encounter, such as a body of water, the handler has the opportunity to guide the dog through problems under controlled conditions. For example, a dog encountering a stream in the middle of its search area may stay focused on the water simply because scent has a tendency to stay in moist areas, becoming even stronger at times. In training, the handler can allow the dog to work with the scent problem for awhile, and begin to understand the dog's perspective of what is happening. Then, if the dog becomes confused, the handler can guide the dog to the other side of the stream to show that the scent continues beyond the stream.

The Training Atmosphere

The atmosphere created around training exercises should also mimic the conditions the dog team will encounter on actual missions. Atmosphere includes the circumstances and conditions under which the team plans to work. Although it's fun to train on sunny, warm days under blue skies and gentle breezes, these are not the conditions of most searches.

Weather is frequently a factor when people get lost in the wilderness, as well as in avalanche rescues and disaster work. Therefore, training should take place during inclement weather as well as during beautiful weather. Training is the best time for a dog team to become familiar with one another's capabilities under the stress of difficult weather. Training at night is also important. Watching a dog work in the light of the day is very different from what a handler is able to see and read from the dog at night. Training at night gives the handler the opportunity to get to know how the dog sounds while working, because visual cues are impaired. Working at night also challenges the dog to continue to work at a normal pace, even when the handler is not clearly visible and the dog is unable to see the surrounding area clearly.

People often believe that variations in wind patterns only affect dogs that air scent and don't affect the way trailing dogs work. In fact,

---

✧ SEARCH BRIEF ✧

Many dog handlers use a piece of flagging tape or a puff bottle with powder to monitor the direction in which the wind blows. As the dog works, the handler holds the flagging tape at arm's length to see where the scent has most likely settled or where the scent may be blowing. To get an accurate picture of how scent is moving at the dog's level the flagging should be held at the height of the dog's nose. A puff bottle simply requires the handler to gently and quickly squeeze the bottle to see which way the powder blows. Puff bottles are used in areas where the wind velocity is mild and during searches in buildings.

Water search training begins in shallow depths close to the shore.

wind affects scent on the ground as well as in the air. Terrain features combine with wind patterns to create exciting opportunities that challenge even the most experienced handlers and dogs. The behavior of wind around and through various terrain features poses many problems that are excellent for training purposes.

Noise

Another element to consider when training is noise and its effect on the dog's ability to concentrate. The sound of thunder and wind blowing makes some dogs nervous, so it's best to get the dog accustomed to these conditions while training. Novice handlers sometimes mention that their puppies have a difficult time concentrating while people are talking. Training exercises provide the best opportunities for a young dog to become familiar with search condi-

tions where people talk with each other and call for the lost person.

The dog also needs to stay focused on its job when crowds are present and watching, and with other searchers approaching, leaving, or working alongside the dog team. Other sounds encountered on searches are whistles being blown to attract the attention of the missing person, and helicopters flying overhead. Gunfire may even be a distraction and threat during hunting season.

Equipment

Most of the equipment used for training a search dog is also used on actual missions, so the investment in good equipment for training is well spent. Handlers can learn what types and brands of equipment work best for them and their dogs through direct experience during training exercises. Because handlers carry all the gear in a backpack, it's to their advantage to understand the purpose of each item and to be as efficient as possible. The items described here are basic items used in wilderness training. Special equipment for more specialized training may also be used once the dog and handler move to a more advanced level.

Training Equipment for the Dog

Equipment for the dog consists of several items that can be used in a variety of situations. The dog should wear a flat collar with an identification tag at all times. Dogs who work in collapsed buildings or rubble piles do not wear collars, however. In these situations a collar is dangerous because it may get caught on loose debris and place the dog in further danger.

A six-foot lead should also be available for when the dog is approaching or leaving the training site or mission base. Even though the dog is under voice control, other circumstances can't always be controlled, so the standard six-foot lead should be used when walking the dog to the start of the problem. Most areas available for training dogs require that dogs be kept on the six-foot lead when not working.

In most disciplines, search dogs wear a non-restrictive harness and/or vest during training exercises and on missions. The harness acts as a signal to the dog that it is working. It should be removed immediately after each exercise has been completed. This reinforces the concept that the dog is working while wearing the harness.

Other items may be attached to the harness, as long as they don't get caught on vegetation or interfere with the dog's ability to move freely. For example, light sticks or reflective lights are used when the dog is working at night. The light is generally attached to the harness and should shine from the top and/or side of the dog. Wherever the light is placed on the dog, it needs to be visible to the handler from various angles. Although the handler wears a headlamp while working at night and usually walks behind the dog, making the dog easier to see, there are many situations in which the dog works on either side or uphill of the handler and so is out of the range of the headlamp.

A handler prepares her puppy for training by dressing the dog in her harness.

In many regions, search dogs wear bear warning bells. The *bear bell* has multiple uses. It creates noise that causes most bears to leave the area where the dog and handler are training or searching. It also notifies the missing person that the animal coming toward them is friendly. Air scent dogs sometimes work at a substantial distance from the handler and can be tracked by the sound of the bell. The bear bell should be attached to the harness where it's not ringing next to the dog's ears.

In addition to the six-foot lead, a 30-foot lead is used while working during the early stages of training. Some dogs work at the end of a 30-foot lead throughout their search careers in wilderness search and rescue. The 30-foot lead attaches to the

A long lead is an important piece of equipment for trailing dogs.

metal ring on the back of the harness, enabling the dog to work comfortably without feeling any restriction around the neck. The use of this training lead is described in more detail later in this chapter.

Vests specifically designed for search and rescue dogs may also be used while training, as well as during searches. Usually bright red or orange, vests identify the dog as a search dog and are visual cues to hunters indicating that the animal in the underbrush is not game. Some dog vests are designed with reflective tape that shines at night to further assist the handler in finding the dog in the dark.

Bowls for water and food are critical, as is a supply of clean water, even during training. Travel bowls made of water-resistant fabric are very convenient because of their light weight and design. Fabric bowls can be folded to the size of an envelope and hooked onto the outside of a backpack. Whether using a fabric bowl or a solid bowl, it's important to keep it in a convenient place so the dog can be watered frequently while working. The dog should be offered water before, during, and after an exercise to stay hydrated.

Dog booties are also used in some areas and situations and should also be kept available. The purpose of booties is to provide extra protection while the dog works in snow, gravel, or among cacti. They can also be used to protect the dog's paws on longer hikes in rough terrain. The dog needs to be comfortable working while wearing booties, so should be introduced to them early in the training. As with every piece of equipment, booties should be associated with fun experiences.

Many dogs adore toys and may look for a toy as a reward after each exercise. If the dog shows a fondness for a particular toy as a reward, it should be stored with the rest of the dog's equipment and be kept available as a reward or prize. Even if the dog prefers other forms of reward, such as praise or food, a toy can be used to provide a break after exercises or to relieve stress during breaks. Of course, the toy should be one the dog enjoys playing with and looks forward to receiving.

Training Equipment for the Handler

The equipment dog handlers use during training is aimed at maximizing their effectiveness as both trainer and dog handler. All the equipment used in training a search dog can also be used on actual search missions, although the manner in which some of the items are used may change on actual missions.

Pack

Either a backpack or a lumbar pack may be used while training a search dog, depending upon how much equipment is required for a particular exercise. Whereas a backpack rests on a person's shoulders and is supported by a waist strap and, in some cases, a chest strap, a lumbar pack rests on the lumbar

Wilderness search dogs often work in orange or red vests for identification.

region of the back and is supported by a waist strap alone. Many handlers prefer using lumbar packs during practices because they are lighter and generally easier to handle. The inventory carried in the pack may be minimal in some training situations

---

✦ SEARCH BRIEF ✦

Training equipment for the dog:
- flat collar
- identification
- 6-foot lead
- non-restrictive harness
- light sticks, a bear bell
- 30-foot lead
- bowls for food and water
- search dog vest
- dog booties
- dog toy.

---

where the weather is mild and the training site is close to parked cars or other conveniences. However, the dog's equipment should always be available in the pack, along with plenty of water for the dog and handler. The pack should be big enough to carry extra clothing in case of dramatic changes in the weather.

Whistle

Many handlers use whistles to call their dog when it works farther away from the handler than the handler's voice can carry. One style of whistle many handlers like is that used by sheepherders to signal commands to their dog. The sound carries and, with practice, variations in the

Dog booties protect against cold snow and rough ground cover.

sounds can be used to communicate different messages to the dog. Whether or not it's used to call a dog, a whistle is a standard piece of equipment for all searchers to attract the attention of the missing person. Therefore, if a whistle is used to attract the dog's attention, it must make a sound that's easy to distinguish from whistles used by other searchers.

Water and Food

Water is a critical element when training a search dog. It's extremely important that the handler and dog remain hydrated to work effectively, continue to work, and stay healthy. If the training area is set up close to cars or other conveniences, it's still necessary to carry enough water for the dog team for the duration of the exercise.

All dogs should be offered water at the start of every training exercise and frequently during the exercise. Larger breeds of dogs require more water. The handler should also drink frequently during the exercise.

Enough food should be carried to replenish the dog team if the exercise becomes prolonged. Generally a search dog does not eat while training. However, if the practice session lasts several hours it may be necessary to take a break and eat something in order to maintain the right level of blood glucose for energy.

Maps

A map is a critical piece of equipment for a canine search team. In wilderness search and rescue topographic maps are used that chart the topographical features of an area and show elevation. A map may be the only source of information about an area, so it should be handy at all times.

Part of a handler's training should include *orienteering* or map and compass reading. Handlers need to be able to pinpoint their location at any time while the dog is working. They also need to be able to determine the best route into and out of their assigned area. A dog handler also uses the map to identify the location of the lost person to command base after the dog pinpoints the person's location. It is sometimes necessary to have several maps to cover a large area because the dog may move across sections charted on more than a single map.

Compass

Part of orienteering is learning to pinpoint locations and features on a map with the aid of a compass. In addition to being a tool to read a map efficiently, a compass also enables a dog handler to communicate the direction of the wind to others. The compass should always be available, so most handlers generally keep it around their neck on a cord called a lanyard. Maps and a compass are the most reliable tools for determining location and direction when no terrain features are outstanding in an area, although a global positioning system may also be used.

Knowing how to use a map and compass is critical for all wilderness search missions.

A Global Positioning System (G.P.S.)

A global positioning system, or G.P.S., is used in search and rescue and can also be a very valuable training tool. A G.P.S. relies on satellite technology to display the location of the individual carrying the unit. The unit described here is about the size

---

✢ SEARCH BRIEF ✢

The type of compass used in search and rescue is a handheld, liquid-filled model with gradients of two degrees and a reflector mirror. A compass with an adjustable declination scale is highly recommended to conveniently adjust for the difference between magnetic north (which is the orientation of a compass) and true north (which is the orientation of maps).

A global positioning system or G.P.S.

data from both the subject's and the dog team's G.P.S. units can be transferred to a computer program and printed on a map of the area. The dog team can then see precisely where they searched in relation to where the subject hiked.

A G.P.S. is also an effective tool when training an air scent dog. The location of the subject can be marked as a waypoint in the G.P.S. unit either before or after the dog team trains. As the dog works, a G.P.S. can be securely attached to the dog's harness. Once the exercise is completed, the pattern is transferred into a computer program along with the location of the subject. A map can be printed with the exact working pattern of the dog. Wind directions can also be noted in the program, as well as the location of clues found.

Although valuable, a G.P.S. does not replace a map and compass, because G.P.S. devices are not 100 percent accurate. One reason is that it's not always possible to register a signal from a satellite. Also, in some locations, such as drainages or under dense tree growth, the device is rendered virtually useless because it can't pick up a signal from a satellite. Weather fronts may also affect the accuracy of the satellite signal. For these reasons, a map and compass should be available as another means of charting an exercise.

of a cell phone. The G.P.S. receives signals from multiple satellites as they orbit the Earth. The unit then calculates the location based on the signals received. Handlers should learn how to use these devices for training purposes as well as on actual missions.

One type of training scenario where a G.P.S. is valuable is for an advanced trailing dog. The individual acting as the lost person, or subject, carries a G.P.S. with them when they hike the pattern they're setting up for a trailing dog. When the dog team searches, they also carry a G.P.S. to chart their exact path of travel. The

Headlamp

Once the dog and handler become more experienced at training in daylight, they're required to participate in training sessions at night because many, if not most, searches occur after dark. For this reason, a headlamp is necessary. Many styles are available. A headlamp is battery powered and lightweight, so it can be worn on the dog handler's head. A functioning headlamp makes it possible to see at night, leaving the handler's hands free to do other things.

Radios

Radios provide communication between the dog team and other team members during a training exercise and on actual searches. Radio protocol is a necessary skill the dog handler must learn. Because of the distance traveled during advanced search training scenarios, it's a good idea for the handler to be able to communicate with someone who knows the location of the subject and/or to be able to speak directly with the subject.

The small walkie-talkie types of radios are able to transmit across a relatively short distance and may be sufficient for training, but they are not adequate for actual search missions. Many handlers prefer to have a radio with a stronger frequency that they can use for actual missions, as well.

Flagging Tape

Handlers often use flagging tape or a puff bottle as a tool to monitor wind direction. The flagging tape referred to here is the lightweight plastic tape available in hardware

✦ **SEARCH BRIEF** ✦

Training equipment for the handler:
• a pack
• a whistle
• water and food
• maps
• a compass
• a Global Positioning System (optional)
• a radio
• a headlamp for night searches
• flagging tape to mark the trail and monitor wind direction, or a puff bottle to monitor wind direction where breezes are calm or non-existent.

stores. It comes in a variety of bright colors and is visible at a distance against different backgrounds. The subject who's laying a trail for a trailing dog's practice session can also use flagging tape to mark the trail. In this application, the tape is tied to trees and shrubs to indicate the direction the person travels and any turns in the training exercise.

The Long Lead

A 30-foot lead is included in the training equipment inventory of the search dog. The long lead has multiple uses in training and search missions, and is used specifically for trailing dogs. It should be made of a lightweight canvas or nylon material. It must be easy to manipulate and manage, because it will easily

Trailing dogs may work on or off a long lead, while air scent dogs always work off lead to be free to work in broad grid patterns into the wind.

become tangled in underbrush and around trees in terrain with more dense vegetation.

Many dogs work off lead in wilderness search and rescue while trailing, although others may work on lead throughout their careers. Because the lead has such an important role in a search dog's training, its purpose should be understood. Attached to the ring on the top of the harness between the dog's shoulders, the long lead is used to guide the dog as it begins to use its nose to find people. The long lead is dis-

tinguished from other leads in that it's never used to make the dog walk at the handler's side in the heel position. This is so the dog associates the long lead with the ability to move freely in all directions and lead the handler.

The purpose of the long lead is to give handlers control over the dog in the early stages of training, and to minimize the need to use their voice to direct or correct the dog's activity. The lead is used to assist the trailing dog while learning to work carefully while focusing on the strongest area of scent. Many beginning search dogs will attempt to chase the scent by running in circles or weaving in wide arcs to the edge of the scent as it blows in the wind. By keeping the beginning dog on lead while it's trailing, the dog is encouraged to stay focused on the path and direction of the strongest scent while the handler walks directly behind. The pace of the dog can also be directed using the long lead.

Most dogs try to work fast at first and run to get to the subject quickly. Using the lead to limit the speed at which the dog works teaches the dog to move at its handler's pace. It's surprisingly difficult for a novice handler to refrain from running in an effort to keep up with the dog when they're just beginning. The enthusiasm of the dog is wonderful and should be encouraged but the dog's pace must be adjusted to accommodate a realistic pace for the handler. By controlling the speed at which it works, the dog learns to monitor the

This trailing dog has been taken off the lead too soon in training; he's following fringe scent that's blown into the rocks and not the strongest scent.

Maintaining tension on a long lead helps the trailing dog learn a steady pace that matches the handler's.

steady pace of the handler. It's unrealistic for a handler to try to keep up with the dog. In fact, it's not possible to run through the wilderness while carrying a backpack, reading a map, talking on the radio, and watching a search dog work.

The dog should never be jerked or forced with the long lead. Rather, as the dog follows the path of the scent, it's the job of the handler to stay behind the dog. If the dog waivers too far from the scent, the lead may be used only to gently guide it back to where the scent should be stronger than in the current location. Guiding with the lead is done fairly early in training and does not continue after the dog understands how to figure out where the scent is strongest and take the handler to the source.

Managing a long lead takes a combination of talent, coordination, and skill. In the early stages of train-

ing, the lead should be coiled so the distance between the dog and handler remains short—no more than six feet. As the dog becomes more confident and adept, the distance between the dog and handler can be gradually lengthened until the lead reaches its full 30 feet. The handler needs to learn to adjust the lead length to accommodate the terrain, vegetation, and responses of the dog. It's best to avoid jerking the lead or allowing it to become tangled in any way that would interfere with the dog.

As the dog and handler become more confident in one another's responses, the handler may consider whether the lead should be removed. Initial stages may include dropping the lead occasionally and allowing the dog to drag it while working. The lead can also be removed periodically rather than all at once. In this way, the dog is weaned from the lead gradually. This also gives the handler an opportunity to observe any changes in the dog's behavior once the lead is removed. Some dogs work well on lead, but once it's removed they may run too fast to be able to work carefully and may lose concentration or begin to play rather than work.

Another problem to watch for when the lead is removed is whether the dog has difficulty pinpointing

The long lead can help the dog focus on the strongest scent during the first year of trailing.

where the scent is stronger and, as a result, runs everywhere the scent may have blown. The lead often helps calm the dog and keep it focused on a smaller area where the scent is stronger. Being able to discern the differences in the dog's style of working on and off lead gives the handler the ability to make a better decision about whether the dog can work off lead.

There are advantages to being able to work trailing dogs off lead during search missions. First, the long lead is one more piece of equipment to manage while working the dog. Many wilderness areas make handling a long lead difficult at best, and the line can easily become tangled around the dog, around the handler, in underbrush, or around tree trunks. Also, without the lead attached, there is less risk that the handler will influence the dog's decisions by tugging or pulling on the line. The dog, not the handler, needs to be leading the direction of the search.

If the plan is to ultimately remove the lead, there are certain things to look for that indicate the dog is ready to work off the lead. The search dog should work confidently with minimal guidance from the handler. In fact, the guidance at this point should be limited to quietly encouraging the dog verbally while the dog works. The dog should be able to stay focused on the task and not need to be pulled back to the scent trail. By the time the lead is removed the dog should also be able to confidently work out problems, such as turns and conflicting scent, on its own. Once the lead is removed, there should be no change in the dog's capabilities, unless it's that the dog is able to work more confidently.

The 30-foot lead should always be kept available for use when required on search missions. Either an air scent or a trailing dog may be in situations where its safety could be at risk and the lead needs to be attached for caution. In situations where the scent blows into swift-moving streams or rivers, or crosses major roads, it's wise to put the dog on the long lead while it continues to work. The dog can continue to follow the scent and stay safe. For this reason, a dog that works off lead needs to be equally willing to work while the lead's attached.

Searching along a stream.

Training Log

The progression a dog team makes throughout training should be documented, for several reasons. A training log gives handlers a record of the various situations encountered. It also gives them a way to review their own and their dog's responses to problems encountered, as well as document the dog team's progression. In addition, a training log may be used to qualify a dog team's capabilities, if needed, for legal purposes and as qualifications for expert witness status in criminal cases. The sample of a trailing dog's training log on page 80 incorporates information for a trailing exercise.

Summary

A good training program provides focus for a search dog's natural abilities. Through training, dogs learn to follow a specific scent and locate clues while ignoring other scents. Training also provides opportunities for handlers to learn about their dog and develop skills and understanding to help their dog succeed. Training should prepare both the dog and handler to work effectively as a team while building confidence and trust in one another. To these ends, training is a fun and exciting process of discovery for the canine search team.

Training Log

Date/Time: June 1/10:00 A.M.   **Dog:** Isis   **Discipline:** Trailing

Handler: Angela   **Support:** Mike   **Subject(s):** Roger

Location: Mount Evans Wilderness

Description of Terrain: Dense forest of pine, aspen. Large rock outcroppings. Elevation gain of 500 feet during trail. Lake in search area.

Weather Conditions: Clear and sunny, cloudless sky. Rain after trail was laid.

Description of Wind: Light wind blowing up mountainside on sunny slopes and down mountainside in the shade at approximately 5 mph.

Description of Scenario: Subject started at a campground and laid the trail at 4 P.M. on the previous day during dry conditions. Heavy rain overnight. Subject walked uphill from P.L.S. and climbed through boulders, circled the lake and walked downhill to a cabin.

Age of Trail: 18 hours

Length of Trail: 2 miles

Wind Direction: Steady from NE

Flagged Trail: Yes ___ No _X_

# of Turns: 6

# of Clues Left: 3

# of Clues Found: 2

Description of Contamination: Campers, elk, 5 hikers at the intersection of 2 foot paths, a family at the lake during the search. Unknown contamination overnight.

Evaluation: Isis established a clear direction of travel at the campground. Followed scent directly uphill and worked scent around the rocks. Found the subject's glove among the rocks. Dog noticed elk on trail and responded when told to wait. Wind was blowing up mountainside and dog followed scent up to ridge, cutting one corner of the subject's trail and missing 1 article. Dog picked up actual trail on ridge top and turned left toward lake. Dog circled the lake and indicated subject's hat at intersection of trail from the lake. Dog made a sharp right turn working for another 1.4 mile to the cabin where the subject was found. Dog worked well through contamination and responded well to command to wait at elk. Dog seemed to notice scent from clue #2 but was intent on the trail, so did not follow up on indication.

Chapter Six
Air Scent

A ir scent dogs are not concerned with the route the missing person took, because they're looking for the missing person's current location. Locating scent in the air as it's sloughed off from its source enables the dog to locate forensic evidence, cadaver material, or the missing person, all at their current location, regardless of how the person or the material got there. The dog's job is to determine if the missing person or evidence is or is not in the dog team's search area.

As scent emanates from a person and evidence, it forms a cone, called a *scent cone,* over some distance as the minute particles of scent disperse. This scent cone is the zone in which an air scent dog is able to detect a person's scent and follow it to find the person. When air scenting, a search dog's nose can cover more area in a few hours than several people searching on foot could cover in one day. In order to search the largest amount of space possible, an air scent dog handler generally moves the dog in a grid pattern across the search area and into the wind.

Air scent dogs work with their heads and noses in the air in order to detect the scent directly from the missing person. When they detect the scent, they often lift their heads higher as if at attention. This response is referred to as an *alert,* which is the trained indication that the subject's scent has been located. The alert is a clear signal to the handler that the dog has pinpointed the scent's source and is prepared to follow it to

An air scent dog works with its head and nose high while trying to locate scent.

a conclusion. The dog then runs toward the source of the scent, often continuing a grid pattern as it finds the edges of the scent within the scent cone. If the wind shifts and the dog loses the scent, the team usually continues to work in their grid pattern from the new direction defined by the activity of the wind. Mature air scent dogs will frequently move independently to find the new location of the scent cone and continue searching to identify the highest concentration of scent within the cone.

Mission Requirements

An air scent dog is an outstanding resource under many search mission conditions and circumstances. The air scent dog team is assigned an area to search in wilderness searches and, because the team works in an assigned area, more than one air scent dog team can work simultaneously on a mission. In fact, multiple air scent dog teams deployed on a wilderness mission are often assigned to work in adjoining areas. They are usually placed where there is a high probability of finding the person, simply because air scent dogs can cover such a large area quickly.

An air scent dog is influenced by the direction in which the wind blows, as well as the prevailing wind and temperatures, which influence how scent is carried by the air across areas or through natural or manmade channels and around obstructions.

This is explained in greater detail in Chapter Four, Scent Dynamics. If the dog team is asked to search an area where there's a cliff, the time of day and the direction of the prevailing winds will determine whether the handler chooses to take their dog to the top of the cliff or to the bottom. If the sun is on the cliff face and the air is warm, the scent will rise, whereas if the cliff is in the shade and the air is cool, as in the evening, the scent will settle to the ground or on vegetation.

Unlike trailing dogs, air scent dogs do not require an identifying scent from a scent article to begin their assignment. An air scent dog may be told to locate any person in the area. However, it's usually advantageous for the dog to have the particular scent of the missing person. Being able to use a scent article to focus on the missing person's scent may save time, and certainly energy, because the handler isn't required to eliminate everyone the dog comes into contact with on a search mission.

Another advantage to using air scent dog teams on a wilderness search mission is the fact that an air scent dog is not concerned as much about residual scent that ages and consequently deteriorates over time. The dog team may be deployed on a search that spans days, weeks, or even months. The passage of time doesn't alter the assignment, which is to find the current location of the missing person.

Conversely, an air scent dog trained to locate and identify forensic evidence is searching for residual scent, because the body, tissue, fluid, or article containing human scent may no longer be apparent in the search location. In these situations, the dogs search for the location of any residual scent from decomposed human tissue or fluid and pinpoint the location of the strongest scent, which remains viable long after anything is visible, even when mixed with soil. A dramatic example of air scenting to residual scent is that of human remains detection when cadaver dogs search old cemeteries. The dogs can and do identify where people are buried in unmarked graves, such as paupers' fields or burial sites from the Civil War.

Air scent dogs can also be trained to detect and identify any clues or articles left by the person for whom the dog is searching. Anything a person touches appears to be imprinted with their unique scent; therefore a search dog can be trained to use a *trained indication* such as sitting, barking, or lying down, to show the handler that the object came in contact with the missing person.

Determining that the missing person is not in an area is yet another valuable way in which air scent dogs are used on search missions. This is known as *clearing an area.* For example, when an air scent dog team is sent into an area of immediate concern, such as a river valley, it's to determine whether the missing person is in the river. If the dog shows no indication of any human scent in the river, it's considered highly probable that the person is not

there and the focus of the search can move to other areas.

The Air Scent Dog

An air scent dog works most effectively off lead. Because the dog moves in grid patterns as it searches for scent in the air, the dog must be able to move freely across and through the search area. Even after scent is detected, the dog must still be able to run quickly and steadily into the scent cone to get to the person. In areas where wind direction varies from moment to moment, it's critical for the dog to be able to work unimpeded before the direction of the wind changes and the scent vanishes.

Because the air scent dog works off lead, it must be under voice control from a distance. Voice control is important because a search dog is not always in the handler's line of sight. Mentioned in the list of training equipment, many handlers use whistles to control their dogs at a distance because their voice doesn't carry as far as the sound of a whistle in the wilderness. Hand signals are also a valuable way of communicating with the dog when sending an air scent dog in a specific direction while it is working at some distance from the handler but is still in visual range.

The areas in which air scent dog teams search often cross other dog teams' areas, or two areas may overlap. For this reason, the dogs must not act territorial when they come into contact with other search dogs. Because the dogs tend to work away from the handler, their responses may not always be monitored in these situations. This is another example of why a search dog's behavior must be reliable; search dogs should not act defensive when encountering another dog on a search.

The areas assigned to air scent teams are often several miles into the wilderness, so they often must hike many miles before beginning their assignment. Therefore, an air scent dog should be energetic and have reliable stamina. It must also be highly motivated to search, especially when there's no indication that the missing person is in the area or the dog locates the person but for some reason is unable to reach her.

Even when the dog team has detected the subject's scent and the handler has been able to identify their approximate location on a map, another search team may be closer and reach the person first. Pinpointing the location of the person is a significant contribution by any search dog, but the dog may be left feeling frustrated at not being able to complete the search by getting to the person.

Dog handlers have sometimes noticed that their search dogs may also react to the scent of a dead body by becoming upset. Wilderness search dog handlers sometimes see the difference in their dog's behavior when finding a recently deceased body where no blood is present, compared to one that's decomposing or bloody. A recently deceased

victim might evoke the same behavior as a live victim, whereas a body that's decomposing or bloody may evoke distress, seen as crawling or whining. Avalanche dogs will often urinate on the snow just before alerting to a victim's body. Search dogs trained specifically on cadaver scent do not react adversely to the scent of decomposing flesh or blood, because it's another familiar scent source they've been trained to locate.

The Air Scent Dog Handler

The handler of an air scent dog must be able to work with the dog at a distance and when the dog is out of sight. For this reason, handlers should be confident the dog will respond to voice commands. They also need to know the dog will return to them to tell them when the dog has found a person or a clue and take them back to the discovery.

The handler also needs to understand and apply search strategy throughout the search. Whether the mission leader or incident commander assigns the area to be searched or asks for the handler's recommendation, the handler must be able to analyze the situation and determine the best strategy to use while working at that time of day or night. Looking at a topographic map of the area, finding the speed and direction of the wind, and noting the time of day, air scent dog handlers know where they need to place their dog to cover the most space in the least amount of time. Due to the size of the search areas, handlers may need to adjust their strategy throughout the search to increase their dog's chances of locating the missing person. At the same time, if the person is not in the area, handlers must be able to feel confident that the dog didn't miss anything and that the area has truly been cleared.

The Training Model

This section is specifically designed to train a dog to air scent. For the purpose of simplicity, in this book the disciplines of air scenting and trailing are described and trained separately. Search dog teams differ on training methods. Theories and experiences seem to vary and, as yet, there is no national standard for training a wilderness search dog that's been adopted by all wilderness search dog teams. One training model recommends keeping the scent disciplines of trailing and air scenting entirely separate because it's believed a dog will revert to what it first learned. Another recommends training a dog to air scent before trailing and combining the two disciplines for a single search dog, which is known as *cross training*. Finally, another recommends initially training a search dog to trail so the handler has an opportunity to work in close proximity to the dog while the training foundation is established. In this training model, the handlers find a

dog that enjoys trailing stays with that discipline and one that prefers air scenting moves easily into that discipline with a good foundation and without any adverse effects.

Marking the Map

The handler must note the search dog's findings and progress on the topographic map. Handlers must know how to record an alert and make note of any interest in an area or direction. They also need to note the wind direction at the time of the alerts and the location of the alerts on the map. The symbols used to mark alerts may vary among handlers, but generally an alert is marked with an uppercase A and interest may be marked with an uppercase I, both pointing in the direction of the alert or interest. This information gathered by the dog teams is communicated to the mission's leaders. When several air scent teams work together, the information collected becomes pieces of a puzzle. When all the alerts are pieced together on one map, the pieces often form a pattern that can point to the missing person.

Training Exercises

Training a dog for search and rescue should be a fun experience for both the dog and handler. Therefore, the exercises described here should always feel like a game for both partners in the dog team. Praise needs

A puppy begins the runaway problem by watching the subject leave, then following.

It's first necessary to decide on a command for the dog to begin to work. Many handlers use distinct commands for air scenting, trailing, and any other specialty such as avalanche, urban/disaster, human remains detection, or cadaver. Some common commands are "find," "search," "get him," or "seek." Whatever command is used, it should be consistent and be used only in association with searching.

The lessons described in this chapter include basic air scenting exercises for wilderness search, which provide a good foundation for more complex experiences. The lessons are designed to focus on specific search skills mentioned in earlier chapters. Because these lessons are specific to air scenting, the subject should be placed with the wind blowing from behind or in such a way that the dog team works into the wind during the exercises. (The person filling the role of the missing person is referred to as the *subject* in these lessons.)

All search training is based on the dog's progress and comprehension of how to work out the problem. The dog should only progress to the next level of training when it has successfully accomplished the objectives of the previous lessons. It is easy to create variety to teach the objective in each lesson, and this should be done to maintain motivation. Search training, by its very nature, involves solving problems, so it should always be interesting for the dog and the handler.

to be enthusiastic, demonstrative, and consistent, no matter what form the dog's reward takes.

Training equipment includes a map of the training area, a compass, flagging tape to keep track of wind speed and direction, a non-restrictive harness, a bagged scent article, and a toy for the dog. The map is necessary to define the search area for the dog team and enable the handler to become proficient in noting the dog's alerts.

The Runaway

Search training begins with *runaway* problems, where the puppy or dog watches the handler leave and must then run to get to him. The objective is to introduce the puppy to the search command and build on the puppy's prey, hunt, and play drives. In the first couple of training sessions with runaway problems, the puppy may not be inclined to use its nose because it can actually see the handler leave, so it appears to be merely a game of chasing and catching the handler. The handler is responsible for setting up the exercises so that the puppy can move into a position where it's able to catch the handler's scent in the air.

Setting up the Initial Exercises

Runaway problems for air scent should be set up in open areas where the puppy can see the handler as the handler leaves, using the visual cue from the handler. The first few search exercises are built on the game of hide-and-seek, where the handler, to whom the puppy is bonded, runs away, hides, and is discovered by the puppy. After the exercise for the very young puppy (see below), which can be accomplished with only the handler and the puppy, other exercises require a helper or surrogate handler to hold the puppy initially while the handler runs away. The helper or surrogate handler then hides and becomes the subject as the puppy's handler works the dog.

The Runaway for a Very Young Puppy

An initial exercise is one where the handler and a very young puppy are out for a walk and the handler runs a short distance away and crouches down behind a bush or a clump of tall grass until the puppy catches up. As with all search exercises, once the puppy finds the handler, it receives lots of excited praise and is encouraged to play with its toy. This lesson can only be used for very young puppies that are not able to outrun their handlers. Most medium sized dogs can run faster than most people by the time they're three months of age, so the application is limited.

The Basic Runaway

The basic runaway requires assistance from a surrogate handler with whom the puppy is familiar and comfortable. The handler should dress the puppy in its harness and/or vest to prepare the puppy for searching. The surrogate handler then holds the puppy as the handler plays a little with the puppy using the reward toy as a teaser. The handler then says "good-bye" and talks to the puppy and shows the puppy the toy as she walks away. The surrogate handler can excite the puppy too by asking, "Where's she going?" or "What's happening?" because the goal is for the puppy to get very excited as the handler leaves and even wriggle and squirm to run after the handler on its own, without continued urging. The handler and helper must avoid telling

As soon as it reaches the victim the puppy gets lots of happy praise.

the puppy to "stay," "come," or use any other command that would control or confuse the puppy.

It's important to set up this problem so that the wind is blowing toward the puppy and so that the puppy is able to watch the handler. The handler walks in a curve to the left or right of the puppy and into the wind while encouraging the puppy for 50 to 100 feet. During this time, the puppy is restrained by the surrogate handler and continues to watch, while the surrogate handler also encourages the puppy. The handler then moves back in line with the puppy and crouches down behind a clump of grass or behind a tree. At the moment the handler crouches down, the surrogate handler gives

the puppy the command to search, lets go of the puppy and runs along behind to reach the handler with the puppy. The puppy receives a lot of praise and the reward of playing with the toy from the handler. The surrogate handler also praises the puppy.

This runaway should be repeated three times in one session in rapid sequence and in subsequent sessions until the puppy runs enthusiastically to the handler. When it's apparent that the puppy understands the game, training moves immediately to the next phase of the runaway.

Finding the Air Scent
In the next stage of the runaway exercises, the handler walks away with the wind blowing crosswise,

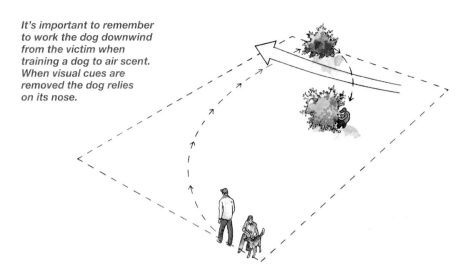

It's important to remember to work the dog downwind from the victim when training a dog to air scent. When visual cues are removed the dog relies on its nose.

across the path of travel. This discourages the puppy from following ground scent too far, because the puppy will move into a position where it can find the handler's scent in the air soon after starting.

The surrogate handler holds the puppy as the handler encourages the puppy to play with the toy. The handler then says "good-bye" and walks away, curving either left or right from the puppy as in the previous exercise, depending on the wind direction. The wind should be blowing across the handler at this stage and toward the handler's path. The handler walks some distance (about 100 to 200 feet) and turns back to get in line with the puppy. At this point, the surrogate handler turns the puppy away from the handler or walks the puppy behind an obstruction. This removes the visual cue of the handler from the puppy's sight.

The handler then walks back in the direction of the puppy to hide behind an obstruction when he or she gets part of the way back to their starting point. The wind should still be blowing across the handler's path of travel. As soon as the handler is in place, the puppy is given the command to search and is released. The puppy will usually run toward where it last saw the handler, but will find the air scent soon after, then run directly into the wind, the air scent, and the handler. When the puppy gets to the handler it receives lots of praise and the reward of playing with the handler and the toy.

This exercise should be repeated two to three times in each training session and practiced several times, increasing the distance slightly once the puppy completes the exercise with confidence and success. When the puppy works enthusiastically and well to find the handler, it's time for the puppy to start searching for someone else, and the handler to start working the dog.

Finding Strangers

When the puppy first begins to look for a subject other than the handler, the person should be someone the puppy knows. Initially, the subject should use the reward toy and play with the puppy before the exercise begins. The handler can then move the puppy behind an obstacle as the subject leaves, no longer talking to the puppy. When the subject is in place, the handler moves the puppy back into the place where the subject left, which must be downwind from the victim's final hiding place. The handler gives the puppy

An air scent dog is shown the scent article to be able to discriminate and find only the victim's scent.

the search command and releases it to find the subject. All commands are delivered enthusiastically. When the puppy finds the subject, everyone praises and plays with the puppy.

This scenario should be set up in different areas and the distance modified so the puppy has several different training situations. Asking the puppy to search through varied vegetation and ground cover is one example of variety. Another is varying the distance and time of day in which training takes place, as well as the hiding place of the subject. As with all exercises, the puppy or dog's progress and understanding of the lesson should determine whether it's ready to move to the next level.

Scent Discrimination for Air Scent Dogs

Some wilderness search teams train all search dogs to scent discriminate from the beginning of their training, whether trailing or air scenting. The value of scent discrimination for an air scent dog is understood when searching on a mission where there are many other people searching in the same area. Scent discrimination can be easily introduced by presenting the dog with an article, or *scent article,* that belongs to the subject in order to imprint the scent while, at the same time, giving the search command to the dog. Scent discrimination is introduced to the dog in an area with no contamination from other people, so the only scent in the area is the scent matching the subject.

When an air scent dog is introduced to scent articles early in training, discrimination is just another tool used by the dog when a scent article is available. Many air scent dog teams do not train their dogs to scent discriminate. For those dog teams, any person found is a subject for their alert, as is any article found (when the dog is trained to indicate articles).

The Area Search

Once the dog has mastered the runaways with and without visual cues and is searching for a stranger, it's time to progress to a more typical area search. In the initial lessons handlers must continue to consider the direction of the wind as they learn to move the dog to where it can eventually locate the subject from a short distance. In the early stages of training beginning handlers need to know where the subject is placed. Knowing this, they can watch as their dog detects and indicates the subject's scent. Handlers also begin to learn how to move their dog in a grid pattern, back and forth across their search area, as they approach the subject or the source of the scent.

Setting up the Exercise

This exercise should take place in a relatively flat, open field or meadow with very few obstructions. The distance worked should be fairly small so that the dog can pick up the subject's scent quickly. The initial training area should be small enough so that the dog detects the subject's scent on the second or third pass in the grid pattern. It's also important to coordinate the subject's path to the eventual hiding place to avoid having the dog follow the subject's scent on the ground instead of looking for it in the air.

The subject and handler use a length of flagging tape or a puff bottle to observe the current wind direction. The handler and subject decide where to work the dog and where the subject will hide, based on the area's topography and the direction of the wind. The subject is then driven to the hiding place and dropped off, or walks to the final hiding place with the wind at his back.

The Search

The handler and dog go to the boundary of their training area, downwind of the subject's final location. Just before starting the exercise, the handler puts the harness on the dog, presents the subject's scent article to the dog (if a scent article is used), and gives the dog the command to search.

With the dog off lead, the handler and dog walk across the length of the boundary as they start their grid pattern. When they get to the edge of the boundary, the handler and dog walk into the wind for approximately 20 yards, then reverse their path and walk back along the width of their search area. This is the beginning of the second leg of their grid.

The dog team continues to walk in the grid pattern, back and forth across the area, until the dog alerts by lifting its head. The handler allows the dog to run directly toward the direction of the alert until they reach the subject. Immediate praise reinforces the lesson quickly, before the dog loses focus. This basic lesson should be done in various locations and situations until the dog works the exercise confidently and consistently. Different subjects should be used to reinforce that the dog is looking for the scent of anyone missing and not just one person.

Adding Distance

In the next set of lessons the dog team covers a larger search area while using the techniques learned in the previous lesson. Scent becomes more dispersed as it moves farther from its source. In this lesson, the dog begins to identify scent from a distance. The handler also begins to look for more subtle signs from the dog that it has detected the scent from farther away.

When the search area is larger the dog has to work for a longer period of time before finding the subject. Another factor in larger areas is the variety of terrain features that influence the behavior of scent, as well as variations in the wind as it blows around these features.

Setting up the Exercise

The search area should be large enough to incorporate terrain features, requiring the dog team to work longer than in the initial scenario. The size of the area should also be relative to the complexity of the terrain. If there are many features in the area, limit the distance the dog is required to search, because the terrain features affect where and how the dog finds scent.

The subject and handler first examine the wind direction by observing how the wind blows the flagging tape. Using this information, the subject determines where in the search area to hide. This information may or may not be shared with the handler. The subject is then driven to or hikes into the area to the final location.

The boundaries of the dog team's search area are shown to the handler, who marks them on the map. The handler observes the wind again to determine where to start the exercise. The goal is to start from a location where the dog can cover as much area as possible to find scent with each pass in the grid pattern.

> ### ✛ SEARCH BRIEF ✛
>
> One goal of air scent dog handlers is to read their dog as it alerts to various scents. Search dogs may show interest in other scents, such as animals, but never alert to or follow the scent. Dog handlers learn to read the dog well enough to determine whether it's showing interest in animals, other people (when scent discriminating), clues, or the actual subject.

An air scent dog handler checks the wind with flagging tape to determine where to move the dog so they can work into and across the wind.

The Search

The dog team moves into the search area, where the handler puts the harness on the dog, presents the subject's scent article to the dog, and gives the dog the command to search. The dog team begins the initial leg of their grid pattern, based on the wind direction.

The handler monitors the direction of the wind by holding a length of flagging tape at arm's length and at approximately the height of the dog's nose, or by using a puff bottle. The handler may need to adjust the direction of the grid pattern to continue to search into the wind.

✦ SEARCH BRIEF ✦

The velocity of the wind and the complexity of the terrain determine the distance between grid patterns. In open areas where the wind is strong, the intervals can be wider because the wind is blowing the scent farther. In areas with dense vegetation and low wind, the intervals should be shorter to ensure that the dog can also detect scent caught among the vegetation while it is working.

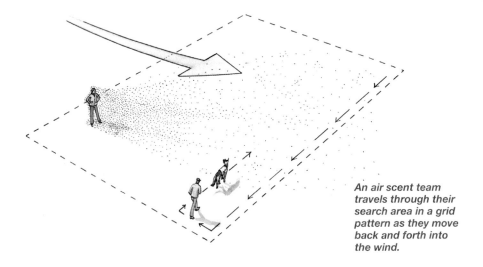

An air scent team travels through their search area in a grid pattern as they move back and forth into the wind.

Scent disperses and becomes weaker as it travels farther from the subject, so the handler should continue to watch the dog for subtle indications of scent from the beginning of the exercise. An *indication* is interest from the dog. This type of indication does not have a trained behavior attached to it, so it's used only to note the search dog's interest in a direction based on scent. The handler guides the dog around any terrain features that could block scent. The team should approach the feature by walking into the wind when possible. It may be necessary to circle the feature at times, especially if the wind swirls around it.

Adding distance to an exercise also adds to the duration of time required, so the handler should keep the dog motivated throughout the problem by moving quickly and deliberately at all times. When the dog locates and alerts to the subject, the handler should run with the dog to the subject.

Larger search areas often require air scent dog handlers to be able to interpret signals from their dog as it indicates scent from farther away. The dog's body language and behavior can convey information clearly and efficiently. For example, a search dog may alert to scent in the area by lifting its head briefly into the wind. In these situations, the scent usually isn't concentrated enough for the dog to be able to follow through to the subject, but it may look into the wind toward the source of the scent. For this type of interest, the handler may want to walk with the dog into the direction of the weak alert to see if the scent becomes stronger. If not, they can keep working in the original grid pattern until they are closer to the source and the scent becomes stronger.

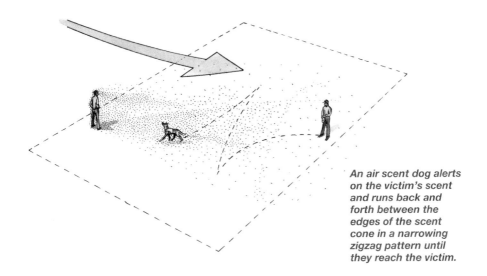

An air scent dog alerts on the victim's scent and runs back and forth between the edges of the scent cone in a narrowing zigzag pattern until they reach the victim.

A *weak alert* is one where the dog's lifts its head in the direction of the scent source. During a weak alert, the dog may only take a few steps in the direction of the scent, but because the scent isn't consistent or strong enough to follow, possibly due to shifting wind direction, the dog is unable to pinpoint the specific location of the subject. In this situation, the handler can move the dog into the direction of the weak alert with relative certainty that the scent will become stronger as they get closer to its source.

An *alert* is one where the dog suddenly and deliberately lifts its head high and runs toward the scent with conviction. The dog may run back and forth in a zigzag as it moves to either side of the scent cone. As the dog gets closer to the source of the scent, the dog's zigzag pattern becomes tighter until it runs to the subject.

The Effects of Terrain

Because terrain features may affect the behavior of the wind and therefore scent, it's important for the dog to be able to perform well in smaller areas before being asked to find someone in larger areas. Exercises in larger search areas give the dog team the opportunity to search through and around the terrain features and changing winds that influence scent. In fact, in many regions of the country, variations in topography in larger search areas mean more complex problems. Variations can include hills, mountains, water, buildings, and open meadows. The

In a multiple victim problem the dog locates the first victim.

air scent dog handler needs to understand how these features affect the dog's ability to find and follow scent. Wind may blow the scent in different directions around the features. The angle at which the dog team approaches these areas may determine whether the dog is able to detect the subject or the article.

There are times when an air scent team makes many adjustments to account for the effects of wind and weather patterns. In larger search areas these influences are more prevalent and affect how the dog handler applies a search strategy. At these times, the value of charting the wind direction and the dog's responses on a map becomes apparent. This use of the map enables the team to remember their search patterns and which areas the dog covered. Charting the

shifts in wind direction may add vital clues that may otherwise be overlooked. In fact, it's possible for one air scent dog to search an area in the morning with no results, then in the evening a second dog team locates the subject while searching the same area under different weather conditions and wind patterns.

The large area exercises are advanced problems based on realistic search situations, and should continue to be varied and modified throughout an air scent wilderness search dog's career. The subject should be hidden in trees, buildings, cars, and anywhere else that could challenge the dog. Any terrain that would typically be encountered on a mission should be the setting for exercises, in all types of weather. As the dog progresses and proves to be consistent with the more advanced problems, it's ready to move on to finding multiple victims.

Multiple Victims

An air scent dog is able to search for a specific individual or several people during the same search. Some examples where a search dog may locate anyone within an area is in an avalanche, on water searches, or following disasters where the dog searches for anyone buried in the snow, drowned, or trapped in a collapsed structure. Typically, no scent articles are used in these situations because the dog is looking for *anyone* in the assigned area. An air scent dog is also ideal when there's a need to find several people lost in the wilderness. On multi-victim searches the handler asks the dog to find *everyone* in the team's assigned area.

In multi-victim training problems, the dog must learn that it needs to continue searching for other victims after it has located the first subject. Everything the dog has learned in previous lessons applies in lessons with more than one subject, except the dog is not presented with a scent article in the beginning and continues to search after the first subject is located.

In this lesson, two subjects are sent into a search area to hide for a single dog team. The subjects should be placed relatively close to each other so the dog can discover the second person soon after the first. However, both subjects should position themselves in such a way as to avoid having the wind blow scent from both individuals toward the dog at the same time or to the same location (for the dog). In other words, the exercises should be set up so that the dog detects each subject's scent separately from different locations in the team's grid pattern.

Setting up the Exercise

A coordinator determines the general area where the two subjects will be placed or are to hide, based on the direction the wind is blowing and the topography in the search area. Both subjects go to their hiding places and make sure they're placed far enough apart that the dog is required to find each separately, based on the direction of the wind. The dog team is given their assignment and told they have more than one subject to find.

The dog suddenly indicates the scent from a second victim.

The dog completes the multi-victim problem by locating the second victim.

For novices, it's helpful when the handler knows how many subjects are in the area. However, it's not necessary for the handler to know where the subjects are located.

No scent article is used in a multi-victim search, because the dog is looking for everyone in the search area. The order in which the dog locates the subjects is not important and is based solely on whose scent the dog finds first, given the direction in which the wind blows the scent to the dog.

The Search

The handler determines the best place to begin by looking at the map, familiarizing herself with the topography, and checking the wind direction and speed. The handler puts the har-

ness and/or vest on the dog and gives the dog the command to search. The team begins their grid pattern.

When the dog locates the first subject, the handler enthusiastically praises the dog just as she would with a single subject. Without removing the dog's harness, the handler moves the dog back into the search pattern and gives the dog the search command again. The dog is usually confused the first time in a multi-victim search, thinking that the training session ends when the first subject is located. The first time this exercise is done, the first subject accompanies the dog team to avoid any confusion.

When the dog indicates the second subject, the handler uses the same enthusiastic praise as with the first subject. The harness and/or vest are removed immediately following the dog's find of the second subject and the handler and both subjects play with the dog.

Learning to Indicate Articles and Clues

Search dogs need to be able to find clues as well as people. *Clues* are articles that have been in contact with the missing person and dropped or left. Clues can also be footprints, but in this lesson the focus is on articles. This skill is as valuable for a trailing dog as it is for an air scent dog. The lesson is designed to teach the dog to locate, identify, and indicate clues in the search area and to determine if an article found actually belongs to the missing subject. The exercises are introduced and taught separately from the dog's victim search training, to avoid confusion with finding the subject.

Setting up the Exercise

Decide how the dog should indicate the articles based on the dog's natural inclinations, such as barking, digging, or sitting. Some situations may prevent certain styles of indication. For example, in law enforcement the dog would be discouraged from picking up the article. In the following training scenario, the dog's indication is to lie down when it finds an article, which is only one possibility.

This scenario is set up as an air scent problem and is also used to train trailing dogs to find articles. Handlers can use their own articles, or another person can set up the scenario for the dog team using articles with his scent. The person who sets up the exercise should avoid walking into the field where the articles are thrown, to prevent the dog from trailing his scent directly to the articles. This is to avoid confusing the goal of finding the article with a goal of finding the owner of the articles. The objective of the exercise is to teach the dog to find, then indicate articles.

Set up the exercise in an open field with access from at least two sides. In this exercise use three socks recently worn by the person who's throwing the socks (they should not be laundered), with a small rock in each sock to weigh it down. The person (it could be the handler) throws each sock into the field and into the wind so they land at least 20 yards apart from one another.

Wait 8 to 24 hours before working the dog to allow any residual scent from the person who threw the articles to blow away. Only the scent emanating from the socks should be left in the field. Because the articles emit scent continuously as they lie in the field, they create a pool of scent, or *scent pool,* in their immediate surrounding area.

The Search

The handler puts the harness on the dog and takes the dog to the starting place, downwind from the socks. Without presenting a scent article to the dog, the handler gives the command to move into the field and search. The dog team begins a normal grid pattern to move into the area where the socks are located.

✛ SEARCH BRIEF ✛

Use objects made of natural material when teaching a dog to find articles. This is because scent adheres best to natural material, such as leather or cloth. As the dog becomes more experienced, it will also be able to find articles made of other material, such as glass, metal, and plastic.

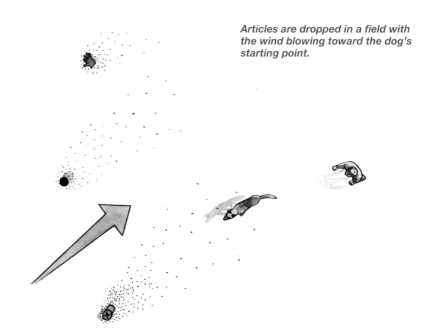

Articles are dropped in a field with the wind blowing toward the dog's starting point.

When the dog identifies the scent of the article and gets to the sock, the dog is praised and given the command to lie down (bark, sit, dig, and so on). The dog may be confused about why it's being asked to lie down, bark or whatever the trained indication might be, so the handler must lavishly praise the dog as it responds to the command. The same grid pattern is repeated and worked in the same way for each article, returning to the starting place each time. Praise the dog every time it finds an article. The dog's indication should also be reinforced every time an article is located.

This exercise should be repeated as many times as necessary until the dog automatically, without fail, performs the trained indication. The dog's response should be automatic

✤ SEARCH BRIEF ✤

The process of teaching a dog how to identify and indicate clues is also used to train dogs for evidence search. In evidence work, a scent article may or may not be used, depending on whether there is a need to find an article with a specific scent or a scent article is available. Sometimes, as in a criminal investigation, a dog may be asked to find any article with human scent that has been left in an area.

Multiple articles are used to teach the dog to locate clues or evidence.

so that there's no confusion when it comes across an article on a search through a large area. Again, this exercise should be introduced sepa- rately and repeated several times until the dog's response is reliable before moving on to finding articles in an area search scenario.

The dog is returned to its starting point and locates the next article.

Searching an Area for Articles

In this lesson, the air scent dog incorporates the lessons learned from the previous exercise into a larger area problem. Instead of finding the person, the goal is to locate the article that belongs to the person.

Setting up the Exercise

A coordinator and/or the handler determines the search area and its boundaries. The subject shows the coordinator the location where she intends to hide the article. The subject hikes into the search area with a large article, such as a backpack, and places the article in the predetermined location. The subject exits the search area before the dog team starts, but leaves the article in place.

The Search

The dog team is given their assignment and may work with or

⊹ **SEARCH BRIEF** ⊹

It's important to note that the subject should always hike into the search area from a point where the wind is at her back. This avoids the problem of an air scent dog picking up the ground scent and trailing instead of looking for the scent in the air. Avoiding ground scent in training becomes a consideration when the dog is being trained specifically as an air scent dog.

---

without a scent article. For training purposes, the handler should be told this is an article search. The dog team moves into their search area, where the handler puts the harness on the dog and gives the dog the command to search. Together they begin the initial leg of their grid pattern, based on the wind direction exactly as they would if they were looking for a lost person.

When the dog locates the article, the handler reinforces the dog's response to the article or method of indication, praising the dog. The dog's harness and/or vest are removed and it receives its reward with lots of playing and excitement.

Finding the Article and the Subject in an Area

In this scenario, the dog team searches for the subject and finds the subject's article *before* finding the subject. The subject will need to evaluate the wind direction and place the article in the location where the dog is most likely to find the clue before it finds the subject.

Setting up the Exercise

A coordinator and/or the handler determine the search area and its boundaries. The subject shows the coordinator the location where he intends to hide the article. The subject evaluates the wind direction and the topography of the search area to determine where the article should be placed in relation to his own location. Once the article is placed the subject goes to a location upwind and some distance from the article. It's important to place the article far enough away from the subject so that the scent from the subject doesn't overwhelm the scent from the article as it blows toward the dog.

The Search

The dog team is assigned the area to work and given the subject's scent article. They move into their search area, where the handler puts the harness on the dog, presents the scent article, and gives the dog the command to search. Together they begin the initial leg of their grid pattern, based on the wind direction.

When the dog locates the article, the desired response is reinforced, the dog is praised, and the article is retrieved. The article should be packaged in a Zip-loc bag for the remain-

der of the search. The dog is then given the command again to continue searching the area. When the dog locates the subject it is praised, the harness is removed, and the dog is rewarded.

Discriminating Articles

For a dog to be able to narrow a search by indicating whether a clue found in the area belongs to the missing person, it must be able to scent discriminate by identifying the scent of the missing person. The ability to scent discriminate enables the dog to determine whether or not the article or clue found in its area belongs to the subject. Naturally, before the lesson of discriminating articles can be taught, the dog must first learn to discriminate scent between individuals, as discussed earlier in the chapter.

The object of article discrimination, or *clue awareness,* is for the

The dog is praised each time it locates an article.

search dog to ignore articles found during the search that have no association with the missing person and only indicate those clues that belong to the subject. The dog's handler needs to know how the dog behaves when faced with an article that is not covered with the subject's familiar scent, as well as how the dog indicates an article that belongs to the subject.

In this lesson, the subject drops one or more articles that belong to her (*the target clue*), and also drops one or more articles that do not have her scent on them (*the decoy clue*). It's imperative that the handler knows which article belongs to the subject and which does not, to be able to reinforce the trained indication when the dog finds the target clue.

Setting up the Exercise

The subject takes at least one target clue and one decoy clue into the assigned search area. The decoy clue can be kept isolated from the subject's scent by placing it in a sealed plastic bag until it's dropped directly from the bag. The subject evaluates the wind direction and places each article in the area in such a way as to ensure that the dog will be able to detect scent from both articles. The subject opens the sealed bag and drops the decoy article directly out of the bag onto the ground. He goes to the other location and drops the target clue. The subject then goes to a location upwind and some distance from both articles and waits.

The Search

The dog team is assigned their search area and begins the exercise using a scent article from the subject. The dog team moves into a starting place, where the handler puts the harness on the dog, presents the scent article, and gives the dog the command to search. Together they begin the initial leg of their grid pattern, based on the wind direction.

If the dog locates the decoy clue, it should not show any identifiable response other than a slight curiosity. When the dog locates the target clue, it should respond with the learned indication from previous exercises and receive ample praise.

Once the target clue is located, the dog should continue to search for the subject. It may be necessary to give the dog the command to search after the article is located. By this time though, dogs usually understand that they're expected to work as long as they're wearing their harness. Once the dog locates the subject, the harness is removed and the dog receives praise along with its reward.

The handler needs to observe the dog's behavior the first few times this scenario is set up. To facilitate this, the target clues should be visually distinguishable from the decoy clues. It can also be helpful if the handler has a general idea of the location of each clue, but it's not necessary. As the dog approaches either clue, the handler watches the dog's behavior to observe whether it ignores one clue and indicates another.

The Find and Refind

It's not enough for a search dog to find the missing person; it must also be able to let the handler know it has been successful. For this reason, all search dogs are trained to alert the handler in some way to their find. Many handlers train their dogs to use a particular signal, or *secondary indication,* that's used only when the dog finds the missing person. Some dogs bark and some run back to the handlers and jump up on them. Some run back and jump on everyone in the search party! Many dogs may pick up a stick to indicate their success and others run back to the handler smiling and wagging their tails. Not all dogs

learn this technique easily and some must be encouraged to be exuberant in their behavior. Whatever signal is used, it needs to be obvious so that the handler understands when the dog has found the person. The dog must then be able to lead the handler back to the subject.

Many dogs trained for wilderness search and rescue are also taught to return to the subject with the handler after initially alerting the handler. Because so many wilderness searches are at night or in bad weather, the dogs are taught to find the person more than once. Known as the *recall/refind,* the dogs are expected to return to the handler to indicate their find, then take the handler back to the missing person. The dog's action must be deliberate and clear to the handler, both when the dog returns to the handler and when it takes the handler back to the subject. The refind requires the dog to be able to find the subject, leave the person, go to the handler, communicate its find to the handler, then get back quickly to the subject. The alert to the handler must be clear and easily read by the handler.

Teaching the refind is best incorporated into regular training sessions following less stressful exercises. One method built into all of the lessons described in this chapter is when the handler runs to the subject with the dog, then plays with the dog as part of the reward. Because dogs love praise and play, most will run back to the handler quickly in order to return to the subject to get their reward. When the dog runs back to the handler in training, the handler can encourage a signal by asking in an excited tone, "Where is she? Did you find her? Show me!" and encourage barking or jumping up. Once at the subject, the handler can also incorporate a particular toy or any stick as the dog's reward, to teach the dog that this object is associated with finding the person. Some handlers have a toy hanging on the outside of their pack for the dog to grab once it has found the person.

If the dog hesitates to take the handler back to the subject, the handler may want to veer away from where the subject is so that the dog

The air scent dog completes the recall/refind by running his handler back to the victim.

must return and get the handler. Often dogs won't return to the handler at first if it's apparent that the handler can see the subject, so it may be necessary for the handler to move out of the dog's line of vision to encourage the dog to seek the handler.

Whatever signal the dog is expected to use, it should be one that's consistent with the dog's personality. A less expressive dog may not be comfortable with barking. A dog that's taught never to jump up on people may not be willing to jump up on the handler during the secondary indication. As with other aspects of training a search dog, the method taught should be determined by the dog's working style.

Summary

Dogs trained in air scenting techniques are a versatile and valuable resource in most search situations. The dogs' energetic enthusiasm gives them the willingness to plunge into the wide variety of circumstances and conditions for which they're called. Once the basics of scenting technique have been mastered, new scenarios can be created by adding new and different problems based on realistic mission circumstances. For more information, The American Rescue Dog Association's book *Search and Rescue Dogs, Training the K-9 Hero* (Howell Book House, 2002), describes their methods for training dogs to air scent without using scent discrimination.

Chapter Seven

Trailing

Trailing is the scenting technique used by search dogs that work with their noses close to the ground as they follow residual scent that settles as a person travels through an area. To review, the scent is blown and may collect on vegetation or among rocks, as well as settling on the ground. Because of this dynamic, the heaviest scent may not be in the exact footsteps where the missing person walks. The behavior of scent and its effect on how search dogs work with it is explained in more detail in Chapter Four, Scent Dynamics.

Mission Requirements

The trailing dog can be a unique and valuable resource in search missions. The key role of a trailing dog is to discover the direction in which the missing person traveled. Starting at the point or area where the subject was last seen, or *point last seen* (P.L.S.), the trailing dog narrows the search area by determining which direction the missing person took from a specific point or area of departure. Ideally, a mission leader will request that the trailing dog team begin searching before other team members begin to search. Based on the trailing dog team's information, other searchers can then be sent into the area identified as the most likely direction in which the person traveled. The dog team needs to be consistent and focused from the beginning of their search assignment to the end. It's important for trailing dog handlers to communicate their findings as soon as possible so other team members can be deployed.

While a trailing dog is determining the direction in which the missing person went, it is also determining where the missing person did not go. This information is certainly valuable in the wilderness, where the possibilities can seem overwhelming. For example, a possible situation is one where the trailing dog searches and moves south from a campground following the person's scent that settled as the person hiked. As the dog follows the scent south, it is also showing that the person did not walk immediately north to a road to possibly drive away in a car.

Of course, it's also the trailing dog's objective to find the missing person, when possible. Search dogs are often asked to respond to a search after someone has been missing for several hours, so it's generally understood that a trailing team will not be able to catch up to someone who hiked for several hours before the trailing team arrived. When a trailing team reaches the missing person, it's usually once the person has stopped traveling and is waiting at some point. More often, the trailing team provides valuable information for other team members to go directly into the correct search area rather than guess about where resources should be deployed.

A trailing dog should also identify any clues along the scent trail. Because the trailing dog is following

A puppy is introduced to the scent article in the first training session.

close to the path the person has traveled, it should be fairly easy to find clues when they're left. Clues can be footprints or any objects the missing person dropped or left along the way, as described in Chapter Six on air scent. The search dog should ignore articles that were not touched by the missing person and should show interest only in those articles that belong to the subject.

The Scent Article

A trailing dog needs to know which scent it is expected to follow. Therefore, an article with the unique scent of a particular person, or *scent article,* is needed to identify that person's scent. The scent article should be made of natural materials whenever possible. Many handlers prefer to be responsible for collecting the scent article, although this is not always possible or practical. Regardless of who collects it, the article's availability can be the critical factor that determines whether a trailing dog can be effective, or even used in a search.

Before the article is presented to the dog, it should not be handled directly by anyone other than the person to whom it belongs. This prevents contamination that could mask the scent of the missing person. The article should be one that was recently used and not laundered. The best way to collect a scent article is to wear gloves. It should be stored in a clean, unused Zip-loc bag. If gloves aren't available, it's also easy to collect the article by turning the bag inside out and picking the article up with the bag as if the bag were a glove. The bag containing the article can then be turned right side out and sealed until needed. As the trailing dog team begins a search, the handler presents the article to the dog which sniffs and sometimes bites it to identify which scent to follow.

The Trailing Dog

A dog used for trailing must have steady concentration and be able to focus on minute particles of a specific scent for long periods of time and over long distances. Trailing dogs search from the moment they're presented with the scent article until they complete the search. Focus is key because there is always contamination in the form of scent from other people and animals whose influence the trailing dog must eliminate, or ignore, while it searches.

A trailing dog also must have the kind of drive and determination that enables it to enjoy the challenge of intricate scent problems encountered during the search. A dog that works carefully and in a measured manner is less likely to miss vital changes in the scent trail, such as points where the lost person turned, changed direction or looped back across his own trail. Because they follow aged, residual scent, trailing dogs need to be able to work carefully throughout the search and be

✦ **SEARCH BRIEF** ✦

Small, convenient scent articles are not always available. Sometimes the only available scent article is the upholstery in the missing person's vehicle. Although not ideal, when it's the only source of scent it a may be used. In these situations, it's best to give the trailing dog access to the inside of the car so it can collect scent from the upholstery. Assuming the vehicle belongs to the missing person, the driver's side in front is the best place to collect the scent.

reliable and consistent in following only the scent of the missing person.

The Trailing Dog Handler

The trailing dog's handler works in close proximity to the dog. Because the dog defines the direction of the team's search pattern and activity, the handler also needs to be patient. The handler of a trailing dog waits for the dog to determine which direction to move as they work out scent problems. The handler must be sensitive to the dog, understanding when the dog needs assistance with a problem, when it's working the actual scent, when it's looking for the scent, or when it's lost the scent.

Trailing dog handlers also look for clues along the trail while they

A trailing dog works carefully and methodically.

the handler is responsible for verifying the accuracy of the trail and communicating that information to the mission leader. Handlers should be aware of their general location at any point along the trail, so they need to consult the map regularly.

The Training Model

This section is specifically designed to train a dog to trail, or follow scent on the ground. Mentioned in the previous chapter is the fact that there are no national standards adopted by all teams for training a wilderness search dog. Whether trailing is an introduction to air scenting, is an additional scent discipline for an air scent dog, or is a separate discipline entirely, the lessons described here are integral to the education of all trailing dogs, although the training methods applied may vary among search teams.

Training Exercises

The trailing lessons described in this chapter cover lessons taught in the first year of training a trailing dog. From the moment a puppy is introduced to the game of search, to working long and older trails with turns and locating clues, the search dog in training learns very quickly when training is a positive and fun process.

Certain items are necessary for training a trailing dog. Equipment includes a non-restrictive dog harness, a 30-foot lead, the dog's toy, a

observe their dog work. Handlers need to be aware of anything their dog finds, as well as footprints or other disturbances along the path. Although a search dog is trained to alert the handler to clues, the handler must be able to interpret and follow up on those alerts, some of which may be quick. All search dog handlers are expected to be aware of clues and trailing dog handlers are in an excellent position to identify valuable evidence in a search while they walk along the path of the missing person.

The trailing dog team's activity and progress are marked on the topographical map the handler carries. Unlike the marks that indicate an air scent dog's alerts, a trailing dog's route is traced on the map while the dog searches. Although the support person may actually mark the map, bagged scent article, and flagging tape tied to metal stakes three feet long. The stakes with strips of flagging tape attached are inserted into the ground as the subject walks away. The purpose of the stakes is to show where the subject actually walks, which is important information for early training.

The handler needs to decide what command to use to tell the dog to start the search. Many handlers use the command "find," and even attach a name, such as, "find Kailey." Another favorite command is "search." Some handlers have separate commands for trailing and air scent problems. Whatever the command used, it should be consistent and only associated with searching.

Each of the following exercises is designed to achieve at least one important training goal. All the scenarios are organized so that the lessons from the previous exercise can be smoothly incorporated into subsequent training sessions. Once the goal of each lesson is achieved, any of the scenarios can easily be modified and used in training and practice sessions throughout the dog's career.

Learning the Game

The objectives of this lesson are to introduce the scent article to the dog, to introduce the search command, and to motivate the dog to look for a person. At least three people are needed for these foundation lessons: the handler, a surrogate handler, and at least one support person. In the beginning, the dog is taught to look for its own handler while someone else (a surrogate handler) actually works with the dog. The handler is the initial subject because the dog is naturally motivated to get to the person with whom it is bonded. After the dog learns the game of searching for its owner, it's a smooth transition to searching for strangers.

When training a search dog to trail, moving to the next level is determined by how consistently successful the dog is in its comprehension of and progress in solving the

A trailing dog and some of the dog team's equipment.

The handler dresses the puppy in the harness for the first lesson.

subject as he walks, and consequently from behind the dog team as they work. The subject should always *walk away from the wind* to avoid having his scent blow into the dog's face while it works. Remember, a trailing dog is being taught to look for the scent on the ground rather than in the air, so the wind should not be allowed to influence the initial phases of training.

The Runaway for Trailing

Taking the dog to the starting point of the exercise, the handler puts the harness on the dog and attaches the long lead to the ring between the dog's shoulders on the harness. A surrogate handler takes the long lead with three feet of lead extended. The surrogate handler holds the dog as the handler walks away in a straight line while placing the stakes into the ground every ten feet.

As the handler quickly walks away, she talks to the dog in an excited voice saying, "I'm leaving," "Good bye," "Where am I going?" and other excited comments to keep the dog

problems presented. The dog should only graduate to the next level of training when it has successfully accomplished the objectives of the previous lessons.

Search training should always be interesting for both the dog and the handler, and motivation is maintained by varying the areas, length, and complexity of each exercise. Trailing requires focused concentration on the part of both dog and handler, so the team should have mastered the principals of the previous problem before progressing. Building a strong foundation is critical to maintaining a positive attitude when problems become more complex.

Setting up the Exercise

The setting for this series of exercises is a flat, open, grassy area with the wind blowing from behind the

---

✤ SEARCH BRIEF ✤

The handler should avoid calling the dog to come or say anything that would quench the dog's excitement, such as "no." Instead, she should talk to the dog in an excited voice while walking away. The surrogate handler can also ask the dog, "Where's she going?"

interested in the fact that she is leaving. The handler walks approximately 50 yards in a straight line and squats down in full view of the dog.

The Search

Starting at the precise point where the handler left (the P.L.S.), the surrogate handler opens the bag containing the handler's scent article and presents it to the dog with a command such as, "find [handler's name]". Allowing anywhere from six to ten feet of tight lead to stretch between the dog and the surrogate handler, the dog is allowed to go to the handler. It's good if the dog is so motivated to get to the handler that it pulls on the lead. The support person picks up the flagging stakes while walking behind the surrogate handler and dog.

As soon as the dog gets to the handler, it receives generous amounts of praise from everyone who's participating, especially from its own handler. Refrain from offering the toy to the dog until the whole scenario is completed. Instead, set up the exercise again right away, starting from the end point of the first exercise. Then repeat the exercise for a third time, starting from the end point of the second exercise.

It's important to remove the dog's harness and/or vest to indicate the end of training and give the dog its toy, along with exuberant praise immediately at the end of the third trail. Play with the dog for a few minutes before ending the lesson.

The second and third time this lesson is set up, the handler may

The excited handler leaves the puppy, using the toy as a teaser for the first runaway problem.

walk a little farther than the last, but no more than 150 yards. The purpose is to establish the concept that the dog is to take the surrogate handler to the person who's leaving.

This initial lesson may be repeated in as few as three training sessions, repeating each exercise three times per session. Remember that the goal is for the dog to be motivated to reach

```
┌─────────────────────────────────┐
│      ✛  SEARCH BRIEF  ✛          │
│                                 │
│   Avoid retracing the trail while│
│  walking back from a training   │
│  exercise with the dog. Instead,│
│  return using another route so that│
│  the dog understands from the   │
│  beginning that its job is to follow│
│  the scent as it becomes fresher,│
│  not older. No backtracking.    │
└─────────────────────────────────┘
```

Initially, the subject's path of travel is marked with stakes and flagging tape while the wind is blowing from behind for a trailing dog. The handler watches the dog's behavior based on the subject's path of travel.

the handler while on lead, so the number of times this lesson is repeated is not as important as the dog's understanding of the objective. This game should be fun and quite easy for the dog at this stage.

There's always a lot of praise at the end of each exercise.

Teaching the Dog to Use Its Nose

The objective of this lesson is to teach to dog to rely on scent to find someone, instead of depending on vision alone. The dog begins to do this naturally as the subject gradually moves out of sight. The requirements are the same here as they were in the first lesson. This series should be set up in three training sessions, repeating each exercise three times per session.

Setting up the Exercise

In an open, grassy field, the handler puts on the dog's harness and long lead and hands the lead to the surrogate handler. The surrogate handler takes the long lead with three feet of lead extended and holds the dog while the handler walks away in a straight line. The handler places the stakes into the ground every ten feet while walking away in a straight line with the wind at his or her back.

The handler walks away while talking excitedly to the dog, saying "good bye!" and keeping the dog's interest on him. The surrogate handler can keep the dog focused by asking, "Where's he going?" The dog should continue to watch the handler walk away and may even pull on the lead and cry or bark to get to the handler. The handler walks approximately 50 yards, this time stepping behind an obstacle such as a bush, rock, or building without making a dramatic turn in his path.

The Search

The surrogate handler presents the scent article to the dog and gives the command to search. Usually the dog pulls on the lead to get to the handler as quickly as possible, so the lead should be kept taut with ten to fifteen feet of distance between the dog and the surrogate handler. If, however, the dog appears to be confused when the handler steps out of sight, the surrogate handler can point to the ground, repeating the command to search. It may even be necessary to take a step in the direction of the trail.

As the dog gets closer to the handler, it may slow down when it realizes it can no longer see the handler. At this point, the dog will usually hesitate, and then drop its nose to the ground as it begins looking for scent. Although this may be a quick gesture at first, the dog is still using its nose to find scent.

When the dog gets to the handler, everyone should praise the dog enthusiastically as a reward for the dog. Repeat this scenario two more times, increasing the trail by a few yards each time, as long as the dog maintains focus and motivation. After the third repetition, the handler removes the harness and/or vest and rewards

When visual cues are removed, the trailing dog naturally relies on its nose.

the dog with the toy, playing with the dog for a few minutes. This exercise should be repeated several times, ideally several times in a week, until the dog confidently gets to the handler without any hesitation.

Limiting Verbal Cues

Repeat the previous training scenario with one change. As the handler leaves the dog, she says "good bye," *but then stays silent while walking away* without looking back. As the dog watches, the handler hides behind an obstacle. The surrogate handler can encourage the dog to watch the handler as she leaves and hides, if the dog loses interest.

Repeat the scenario a third time immediately, adding a little distance to the length of the trail, as long as the dog stays motivated and is successful. The dog should still be able to watch the handler walk away and see her disappear. At the end of the lesson series, the dog's harness is removed and it is rewarded while getting lots of praise for a job well done.

✦ SEARCH BRIEF ✦

The handler should try to position herself so she can watch while her dog works. Watch for changes in the dog's body as indicators of what it's experiencing. These might include facial expressions, ear set, tail set, and pace.

Finding Strangers

The objective of this lesson is to make the transition to searching for strangers while the handler works the dog. The person who walks away from the dog as he lays the trail is referred to as the *subject,* and is playing the role of the missing person. When this lesson is first introduced, one option is for the subject to be someone the dog knows well.

Repeat the exercise described in the previous lesson, with one important modification: Instead of the dog's handler laying the trail, the dog's handler now works the dog while someone else lays the trail. The subject can be a stranger or someone the dog knows. If the dog hesitates to start, have the subject talk excitedly to the dog as he leaves, using the technique set up in the first lesson, and progress through the next few lessons.

Direction of Travel

This lesson introduces the trailing dog to the significance of the point last seen, or P.L.S., and the responsibility of figuring out where the subject went after removing the visual cue. The P.L.S. is introduced as a location previously unknown to the dog. The setting for the following scenarios can include terrain with moderate grades and natural vegetation.

Setting up the Exercise

The dog team and subject walk together to a location where the handler puts the harness on the dog and attaches the long lead. At the P.L.S., the subject says good bye to the dog and, as the subject silently walks away, the handler turns away with the dog so the dog can no longer watch the subject.

The subject walks 100 yards in a straight line away from the wind while planting the stakes in the ground every ten yards. At the end of the subject's trail, she crouches down to become less obvious. She should still be in sight of the dog at this point, but not be obvious to the dog.

The Search

After the subject gets into place, the handler returns the dog to the P.L.S. and presents the scent article. Once the command to search is given, the dog is allowed to sniff the ground to figure out where the subject went. If necessary, the handler can point to the ground and even take a few steps in the direction of the subject while repeating the command.

The dog must work solely with scent, instead of relying on supplemental visual clues from this point forward, although the dog may continue to look for the subject as well. If the dog sees the subject, allow the dog to go directly to her. At the end of the exercise the dog receives abundant praise from the handler and the subject. Repeat the exercise once.

The handler should follow directly behind the dog with enough length in the lead to enable the dog to move to either side of the stakes. The handler should stay directly behind the

---

+ **SEARCH BRIEF** +

It's not necessary for the subject to stomp and scrape her feet on the ground at the P.L.S. to make their scent stronger on the ground. The scent the trailing dog follows is from the skin rafts that have fallen from the subject's body, which aren't influenced by stomping the ground. Also, the trailing dog must be able to detect the various intensities of scent at all stages and not become dependent upon how the subject behaves.

---

dog in a straight line in relation to the direction the dog is moving.

Removing Visual Cues

Once the dog has mastered the basic runaway problem by enthusiastically and consistently finding the subject, it's ready to progress to the next level. Removing visual cues is a key point for the search dog, as it must rely solely upon its nose and ability to find scent to locate the subject. In this exercise, the previous scenario should be repeated except the dog is taken away from the subject before he starts to lay the trail at the P.L.S. The dog doesn't see the subject until the end of the exercise.

The handler and dog hide behind an obstacle while the subject leaves from a pre-determined P.L.S. The han-

Ultimately, the trailing dog uses its nose throughout the exercise to determine the subject's direction of travel.

dler takes the dog to the P.L.S., where the harness and long lead are put on the dog and the scent article is presented with the command to search.

The key difference in this scenario is that the dog begins to work directly from the search command using the scent article to identify the person it's supposed to find. It also must identify and follow the scent at the P.L.S. for the first time and determine where the scent goes.

This scenario can be repeated in the next training session as a way to reinforce the lesson. If the dog has difficulty understanding what it's expected to do, go back to the first scenario in this lesson where the dog has contact with the subject at the P.L.S. before starting. This is preferable to allowing the dog to become frustrated.

Reinforce and Build

Now that the dog understands it must first find, then follow scent to locate someone, it's possible to add varying degrees of difficulty to the lessons. For a trailing dog, these consist of time and distance added to the trail. As more distance is added, the scent ages. As the trail ages, the dog is challenged to stay focused on the scent as it blows around and settles on the ground. In fact, the degree to which a particular problem is considered to be difficult for a trailing dog is often related to how long the scent ages. The increased distance also challenges the dog to concentrate and stay focused on the scent trail for a longer period of time.

Have the subject gradually lengthen the distance of the straight-line trails so the dog gets used to searching over longer distances. Gradually feed the length of the lead out to the full 30 feet as the dog begins to work consistently in these preliminary exercises. The fact that the dog works farther away from the handler should not have a negative effect on the outcome of the exercise, which is why the lead should be lengthened gradually.

Increase the time the scent ages by waiting for a pre-determined period of time after the subject leaves before starting the dog on the trail. Up to this point, the scent trails have been relatively fresh, or *hot trails.* When the dog starts to work immediately after the subject leaves, the scent doesn't have time to blow around, disperse, or dry out. Allow the scent to age by waiting ten minutes before starting, while the subject waits at the end of the trail. Increase the time the trail ages incrementally by ten to fifteen minutes. In the next series of lessons the time the scent ages continues to increase, along with other levels of complexity.

Adding Turns

When a person goes on a hike, their natural pattern of walking is to make turns on the trail. The objective of this lesson is to teach the dog how to resolve scent problems created by turns. At this stage of training the dog should still be on a long lead.

When a person makes right angle turns, the scent usually doesn't travel exactly in the same pattern. Instead, the scent is blown by the wind. Understanding this is the first step toward recognizing how the dog works out scent problems created when a person makes a turn in the trail. When starting out, the beginning trailing dog usually continues to follow scent beyond the turn, or *overshoots* the turn, in an effort to follow the scent. Once it realizes that the scent gets weaker, it should return to the corner of the trail where the quality and direction of the scent changes, and may circle to determine the correct direction of the scent.

Setting up the Exercise

The handler takes the dog out of sight as the subject lays the trail. From this point forward, the dog should not watch the subject as she sets up the problem. The subject lays the trail as in the previous lessons, adding a single, gradual curve to either the left or the right of the initial leg of the trail. The subject inserts the flagged stakes into the ground at regular intervals.

The Search

The handler takes the dog to the point last seen, puts the harness on

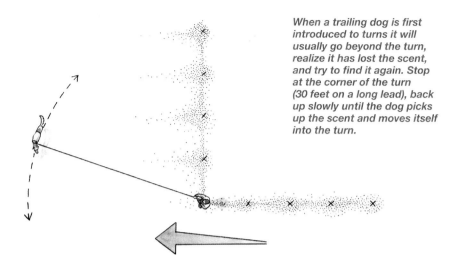

When a trailing dog is first introduced to turns it will usually go beyond the turn, realize it has lost the scent, and try to find it again. Stop at the corner of the turn (30 feet on a long lead), back up slowly until the dog picks up the scent and moves itself into the turn.

the dog, and attaches the lead. The scent article is presented to the dog and the command given. As the dog approaches the curve in the trail, it may go slightly beyond the curve and complete the problem slightly

downwind from where the subject actually walked. Praise the dog enthusiastically when it reaches the subject.

Right Angle Turns

The difficulty of the previous lesson increases as turns become more abrupt, as in right angle turns. The objective of this lesson is to teach the dog to work out scent in these sudden changes of direction.

Setting up the Exercise

The subject sets up the exercise by walking in a straight path away from the wind and inserting the flagged stakes into the ground. The subject lays the first leg of the trail by walking in a straight line for at least 50 yards with the wind at his back. At this point, the subject makes either a right or a left turn, marking the turn clearly with the stakes. A good pattern to use

> ✦ **SEARCH BRIEF** ✦
>
> Make sure the trail is laid with the wind or breeze blowing from behind the subject as she begins laying the first portion of her trail. This prevents the dog from picking up an air scent from the subject as she waits at her hiding place, thereby eliminating the need to follow scent on the ground. The influence of the wind should always be considered when setting up trails for a beginning trailing dog, so the only scent the dog finds is the scent on the ground.

The handler stops when she sees the trailing dog start to look for the scent at a corner.

in marking turns is to insert one stake ten feet before the turn, one stake at the point of the turn and a third stake ten feet into the second leg of the trail or after the turn. The subject continues walking for at least 20 yards before stopping at the end point. The wind should be blowing *across* the second leg of the trail.

The Search

The handler starts the dog at the P.L.S. on lead as before, presenting the scent article and giving the search command to the dog. When the dog reaches the corner of the turn, the handler allows the dog to continue with no change in pace. Assuming the wind is blowing from behind the dog in the direction of the trail, the dog usually continues past the corner of the turn as it follows the scent.

The handler continues to follow the dog until the handler reaches the corner of the turn, which could be as much 30 feet or the length of the lead. If the dog does not return to the

✢ **SEARCH BRIEF** ✢

Many dogs circle as they attempt to find where the scent changes direction at the corner of the turn. Allow the dog to do what's needed to refind the scent and get back to the corner on its own, within the length of the 30-foot lead. To avoid getting tangled, keep the lead off the ground and turn with the lead as the dog circles. The handler should walk backward as the dog returns to the corner.

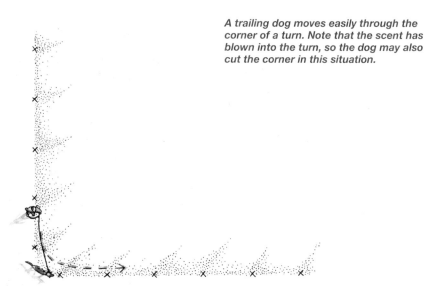

A trailing dog moves easily through the corner of a turn. Note that the scent has blown into the turn, so the dog may also cut the corner in this situation.

corner on its own initiative, the handler silently stops at the corner and slowly begins to walk backward until the dog gets back to the corner of the turn. Once the dog returns to the corner it usually realizes that the subject made the turn, but if not, the handler can point to the ground in the direction of the second leg of the trail to *show* the dog the scent. Frustration can be avoided by limiting the distance the dog is allowed to search beyond the turn. Also, the dog is encouraged to discover how to work through the confusion of turns by itself with only a little guidance from the handler.

If the dog overshoots the corner but finds the second leg of the trail without returning to the corner, allow it to complete the exercise. Even when the dog does not identify the corner, it discovers that scent can

change directions and the dog will be more thoughtful next time while working, understanding that scent doesn't always go in one direction.

Right Angle Turns in the Opposite Direction

The next step is to lay the trail with the turn in the opposite direction from the turn introduced in the previous scenario. Once the dog works well with turns going in both directions, they can be incorporated into every training exercise, as appropriate.

Scent Discrimination

Scent discrimination refers to the dog's ability to distinguish among multiple scents. In this lesson, the objective is to teach the dog to follow the subject's scent and ignore the scent from others, which is referred to as *contamination*. Problems of scent discrimination require at least four people, flagging tape, and the other equipment used up to this point. The scent article identifies the scent the dog should follow, regardless of the other scents encountered. The *subject* is the person who lays the trail, or the missing person, and the *decoy* is the person whose scent acts as contamination for the subject's scent.

Setting up the Exercise

The subject and the decoy lay the trail together. Starting at a single P.L.S., the subject and the decoy walk alongside one another in the same direction for at least 100 yards. Only the subject needs to flag the first leg of the trail. At approximately 100 yards the decoy branches off from the subject's direction and marks the point of his departure using a distinguishing piece of flagging—one that's either another color or two separate pieces of flagging tied next to each other. The subject continues walking straight ahead to complete the problem. The decoy continues to walk away from the subject in a big arc until he has returned to the staging area, where he stays clear of the dog until the exercise has been completed.

The Search

The handler takes the dog to the P.L.S. and gets the dog ready with the harness and lead. The handler gives the dog the command to

search, using the subject's scent article to identify which scent they must find. The dog begins as usual, moving in the direction of both the subject and the decoy.

At the point of departure of the decoy, the dog may show interest in the area where the second scent moves off in another direction, but should go back to the subject's trail to complete the exercise by finding the subject. When the dog gets to the subject, everyone offers lots of praise and congratulations.

Knowing where the decoy branches off gives the handler the opportunity to watch how the dog looks while working through the problem of distinguishing scents that move in different directions. The dogs should be allowed to work out this problem on its own, if possible. The trailing dog may follow the decoy's scent for a few yards before it realizes the subject's scent has moved in another direction.

One of the reasons this pattern is a good one to use when introducing scent discrimination is because the two scents mingle for some distance before separating. When the dog realizes that one of the scents becomes weaker, it must then determine where the subject's scent is and ignore the other scent. This pattern also enables the handler to observe the dog's behavior at the point where the decoy's scent branches off.

If the dog becomes confused and needs help, the handler should back up to the point at which the two scents separate to give the dog an opportunity to find the subject's scent. If the dog still needs help, remind it of the subject's scent by reintroducing the scent article and pointing to the ground in the direction of the subject's trail, beyond

where the decoy branched off from the main trail. The trailing dog should continue to work on scent discrimination and progress to more difficult and complex problems only after it has become completely competent in basic scent discrimination.

Other Patterns for Scent Discrimination

Once the problem of scent discrimination has been introduced and worked successfully, it's important to create a variety of patterns and challenges that require the dog to discriminate between distinct scents. It's also important to make sure no habits or assumptions are formed, such as that the subject is the person who always moves straight ahead while the decoy always takes the detour. Scent discrimination exercises should be incorporated into training for the remainder of the trailing dog's career. Following are examples of how scent discrimination patterns can be set up and incorporated into training.

Have the subject lay the trail, and then have one or several people cut across the trail at various locations. This can be done while the trail's being set up or just before the dog team is ready to work, adding fresher contaminating scent. Several people cutting across the trail at a single location or intersecting the trail in different directions creates another

---

problem. A realistic and important problem to familiarize the dog with is one where several people have been standing and moving around the P.L.S. before the dog begins to search. As the lessons become more complex and advanced, contamination becomes more prevalent as a natural part of each scenario, although this may not always be obvious to the handler.

Articles and Clues

Search dogs need to be able to identify articles left in the search area that belong to the missing person. This lesson teaches the dog how to identify an article and provides an opportunity for the handler to show the dog how to indicate articles that belong to the missing subject. At the same time, the dog is learning to ignore articles that don't belong to the subject. This method is an appropriate way to train either trailing or air scenting dogs.

The first lesson on finding articles and clues described in Chapter Six, Air Scent, is valid for training trailing dogs to indicate clues as well. See the instructions in "Learning to Indicate Articles and Clues" in Chapter Six (page 98). Set up the same scenario without a scent article to teach the dog how to locate and identify clues.

When the dog understands that the handler wants it to find clues as well as the missing person, the lesson can easily be incorporated into regular training scenarios. As the subject lays

the trail, she drops an article with her scent somewhere along the trail. When the dog approaches the article on the trail, the handler praises it and verbally reinforces the response to indicate the clue, such as lying down where the article is found.

Clues and Scent Discrimination

The next step in finding clues is to ensure that the dog is only indicating those articles covered with the scent of the missing person, or the *target clue.* To teach this, it's necessary to set up scenarios in which clues that are not associated with the subject, or *decoy clues,* are also on the trail, along with those belonging to the subject. As in the previous scenario, the subject drops an article covered with her scent as she lays the trail for the dog. The subject also drops a decoy clue on another point along the trail.

In order to maintain the distinctiveness between the articles, it's important to keep the articles with someone else's scent in a sealed plastic bag and drop the decoy articles directly from the bag without touching them. The subject should not touch these articles until after the exercise is completed.

The handler needs to know which article belongs to the subject, so each article should be easy to distinguish by sight. The first few times this scenario is set up, the handler should also know where each article is located in order to observe the dog's behavior when approaching all clues. When the dog approaches the decoy clue, it should act as if it's unremarkable (although the dog may sniff the article out of curiosity) and continue to work. On the other hand, when the dog approaches the target clue belonging to the subject, it should respond with the indication that was taught. The handler should ignore any curiosity the dog has for the decoy clue and praise the dog enthusiastically when the target clue is indicated.

Negative Indications

Negative indications were discussed in an earlier chapter and their application applies to trailing dogs. A *negative indication* is when the search dog determines where the victim did *not* travel. When a trailing dog turns left instead of right while searching for a subject, the handler considers the negative indication to be that the subject did not turn right.

Another application in training is a *negative trail,* where the handler presents the dog with a scent article that does not belong to the subject that the dog is asked to find. As a training exercise, this gives the handler the opportunity to see how the dog behaves when there is no scent matching the article and, therefore, no scent to follow. The dog should first be strong in scent discrimination with contamination before setting up this exercise.

Still another training exercise is that of a *negative find,* where the dog follows the subject matching the scent article, as in a basic trailing exercise, but the scent disappears at some point along the trail. This can be set up with the subject getting into a closed vehicle at a road and driving away. The dog should indicate the lack of scent in the same way it would indicate the lack of scent in the negative trail. For either of these scenarios the handler can teach the dog how to show there's no scent as a trained indication. Some handlers prefer to use a passive indication, such as sitting or lying down. Often the dog will whine when the scent disappears.

Summary

Once the basic foundation for trailing is established, accomplishments from any of the lessons should be combined and mixed regularly to simulate actual search scenarios. Following ground scent requires focus and discipline for both the dog and the handler. Keeping in mind the unpredictability inherent in search missions and the disoriented behavior of people when they're lost, training should continue to provide unexpected situations and new experiences throughout the trailing dog team's career.

Chapter Eight
The Partnership

Both members of a search dog team share a very close partnership. Specific qualities, characteristics, and skills used in the operations of search and rescue are required to be an effective dog team. The special nature of the dog team is another aspect that expresses its unique identity. The close bond between the dog and handler is apparent in how the dog team works together, how they support each other, and their confidence in one another.

Working Together

An effective search dog team is the result of a dog and handler who work well together. This means both the dog and handler work toward the shared objective of locating lost or missing people. Because a well-trained search dog is one of the most valuable resources on a search mission, it's important that the dog be allowed to carry out its assignment free from any unnecessary interference. Dogs, like people, have individual working styles and both the dog and handler must be able to rec-

ognize and work with one another's distinctive manner in order to be effective. Both members of a search dog team begin to learn about one another's styles from the moment training begins.

An example of a particular working style is a dog that moves very quickly and likes to run across large areas as fast as possible while working with its nose in the air to catch scent up high. These dogs are happiest (and therefore most effective) when working air-scenting problems, which require that a dog be able to cover large areas, often running, with its nose in the air looking for and identifying scent as it's carried in the air. When handlers appreciate this manner of working as a strength in the dog, they can adapt themselves to that style and work better with the dog than if they were to demand that the dog work methodically, with its nose to the ground. Forcing a dog to work contrary to its innate strengths risks limiting the dog's effectiveness, and therefore the effectiveness of the team.

At the same time, if a search dog is unable to recognize the handler as part of this partnership or is unable to understand the handler's role, the team will be limited to only what the dog is willing to do on its own without the support of a knowledgeable handler. This limitation could manifest itself as a dog that runs around chasing scent until it disappears or is blown away and a handler who runs around trying to keep up with the dog. This image is one of chaos and offers very little satisfaction or fulfillment for the dog, the handler, or anyone else involved in the mission. When the objective is to help locate lost or missing people, the goal is to discover how this can be accomplished most effectively between the dog team's members.

Close partners enjoy working and playing together.

Supporting Each Other

Not only do the search dog team members need to work well together, but they should also enjoy working with each other. *Support your dog* is a directive often used when search dog handlers advise each other. This means search dog handlers should know their dog's strengths, trust what their dog is communicating to them, and provide their dog with whatever it needs to succeed. A handler's ability to support the dog is developed through a lot of practice and experience over time.

Each time handlers train or practice with their dogs, they have the opportunity to watch how the dogs solve problems. They also gain understanding of the types of decisions their dog makes and the situations that create confusion for the dog or require assistance from the handler. As training progresses, handlers begin to see how their dog works when there's a lot of scent from sources other than the missing person or heavy contamination, for example. Does the dog circle the area? Does it whine and sniff the ground faster? Does the dog stop searching altogether? Once the dog's responses are recognized in training, the handler is better prepared to recognize the signs again and can determine what, if anything needs to be done to help the dog when it confronts the same type of problem on a mission.

Some other examples of the way search dog handlers support their dog are in recognizing when their dog needs water or food and providing the dog with what it needs. One of the handler's jobs is to carry adequate equipment for both team members to not only complete the mission, but also survive in the wilderness for at least 24 hours under a range of possible conditions.

Handlers also must be aware of the circumstances surrounding each training session and on missions, to be able to keep the dog, and themselves, safe. A search dog usually won't be conscious of dangers that could be inherent on a mission. Therefore the dog's handler needs to be aware of these and provide guidance when required. For example, if a dog is searching along a swift-moving river it's always prudent to put the dog on a long lead in case it's compelled to follow scent into the water.

To some degree, the search dog also must be able to support its handler by learning to recognize the handler's strengths and limitations and adjusting its activity to those preferences. An example is the physical difference between dogs and people. Most dogs can move faster than most people, especially when the person is carrying a heavy backpack. It's critical that the dog be able and willing to modify its speed to keep the handler in sight, or return to the handler to verify the handler's location—even for air scent dogs that generally work farther away from the handler than do trailing dogs. When the dog recognizes the handler's limitations (relative to the dog's abilities), it can adjust its pace to keep the team together or run back to direct the handler to its discovery. Doing this demonstrates a willingness to work within the bounds of the handler's limitations and support the team's objective.

Confidence in One Another

As the handler and search dog train and work together frequently and closely, they gain confidence in one another. The principle that search dog training is based on positive reinforcement and praise is also stressed in earlier chapters. Controlled practice sessions, where the members of the dog team can continually succeed and grow through achievement, are critical to developing and building confidence. Search and rescue work can be grueling and emotionally draining at times, so the team members need to feel good about their partnership and the results they can achieve together. There are plenty of opportunities for confusion for both the dog and the handler under the normal circumstances of search and rescue missions, without creating them deliberately in training. Ideally, both the dog and the handler should have the sense that they can always rely on one another, whatever the circumstances.

Knowing how to support the search dog is key to working together well.

The importance of confidence is exemplified in the experience of many trailing dog handlers. On searches where a trailing dog is searching for the scent on the ground, the dog may indicate that the missing person moved into an area that seems impossible, given the profile of the missing person. But, because trailing dog handlers train their dogs to indicate the direction of the missing person's path of travel, they learn to trust that their dog is truly following the correct scent as they work through areas of difficulty. Also, because the behavior of a person who's lost rarely follows the same logic as that of a person who knows where they're going, it's not always easy to understand why anyone would go where a trailing dog might indicate. At the same time, to continue working well, the dog needs to feel the handler's confidence and trust that it will be allowed to continue to work with the evidence gathered. The handler communicates the dog's findings to the mission leader, even when it seems contrary to logic.

All experienced search dog handlers can describe examples of missions where lost people were located far from the area in which they were expected. A mission where this occurred involved an 80-year-old woman recovering from hip replacement surgery and walking with a cane. By the time she was found, she had hiked well over six miles from her last known location. She was located at an altitude of 11,000 feet and had survived three days and nights, in addition to two surprise snowstorms, wearing a nylon jacket, jeans, and sneakers. A confident handler allows the dog to continue working, in spite of the conflicting information, which, in this case, was that this particular woman could neither walk very far nor survive the unexpected winterlike conditions. A dog that feels this level of confidence from the handler will continue to work well throughout its career.

A good way for a team to develop this confidence is by setting up controlled situations in training. In this way, the dog can be confronted by problems that the handler is aware of, enabling the handler to observe the dog under the specific circumstances. If the dog stops working or becomes too confused, the handler can then encourage the dog through the situation with guidance, not force. For more difficult problems, handlers may need to guide their dog to move into a location where they know the dog can work through the dilemma. Either way, the dog deserves a great deal of praise when it resolves the problem, and handlers learn more about their dog's capabilities, which is their reward.

Communication

At the core of an effective, complementary partnership is good communication. Sensitive communication between a search dog and its handler is vital, especially since the lines of communication cross two species. The standard for good communication begins developing when a puppy first arrives in its new home, and continues throughout the life of the search dog team. The focus of communication here is in the context of search missions.

An experienced search dog understands the difference between a practice session and an actual mission. There are several non-verbal cues that indicate the difference, such as the pager going off, the time of day or night, the excitement of the handler, the search gear as it's being loaded into the vehicle, and the drive to the mission. By the time a search dog team is certified to respond to a mission, the dog and handler understand the behavior and protocols expected on search missions. At mission base, the dog is expected to be under control and ready to search. The handler is responsible for conveying and reinforcing a professional

A trailing dog shows where the victim walked and where he did not walk.

A search dog team waits to be briefed before beginning its assignment.

image to the dog. The search dog team can then present a professional image to others. While dogs often play together before practice sessions, on actual missions they're expected to wait for their assignments and begin to work soon after arriving at command base.

The expectations for a dog team on a search should be clear by the time they begin their assignment. Dressing the dog in its harness signals the start of each dog's assignment in a wilderness search. Another indicator is when the dog is presented with the scent article, when available. When the handler gives the dog the command to search, the team should start to work and continue until the person is found or the mission is otherwise resolved. The atmosphere surrounding missions is more intense than training sessions

and can be confusing at times. Nevertheless, the dog team should always project a professional and well-trained image.

There are infinite opportunities to hone communication skills between a handler and a search dog during a mission. Two principal messages the handler receives from the dog are where the scent is found or that there is no scent in the area. When a trailing dog works deliberately to carefully follow ground scent, the handler should have a good idea of whether the source of the scent is the missing person or some other source, such as other animals, which a certified search dog should not follow. As the dog team progresses in their assignment the handler needs to be able to translate the dog's findings over the radio to the mission leader. Some of the information handlers are expected to relay to mission base is their location, their progress, and whether they feel the dog is working the scent in their area. Another piece of definitive information they may offer a mission leader is when the dog fails to pick up any scent.

One key role of an air scent dog already mentioned is that it can clear whole areas of the probability that the missing person is located in the particular area. Therefore, it's expected that an air scent dog handler understands when the dog indicates that it has completed the assignment without finding scent. A mission leader is usually grateful for any assistance in eliminating areas and can move resources into locations where there's a higher probability of finding the missing person.

Trailing dog teams are also deployed on missions where their dogs are unable to locate scent or where the scent has disappeared. Trailing dog handlers need to understand how their dogs convey this information as well. If the trailing dog fails to move in any particular direction and simply doesn't continue to search, the handler needs to be willing to say that the dog did not identify any scent. Although its possible the dog is not able to find the victim's scent at that time, there are also other possibilities that could be explored. One possibility is that the person was in the area but got in a car and left, so further search of the area would be futile.

Another possibility when no scent is discernable is that the dog team

was sent to the wrong location or that the person was never actually in the area in the first place and the information received was wrong. Sometimes the desire to help in a positive way on a mission is so powerful that searchers may run the risk of ignoring what their dog is communicating and hesitate to report that their dog was unable to locate scent. Because their dog is their most reliable resource, handlers need to consider their dog's findings above their own logic, remembering that the dog is able to collect more information than the handler.

Certainly, there are many opportunities for handlers to recognize nuances and signals from their dog while searching. The dog also needs to be able to rely on signals it receives from the handler. The point is to clearly communicate and understand as much of the information relayed as possible, while continuing to expand on that basis of understanding.

Often a trailing dog's behavior changes as it gets closer to the object of the search, the missing person. The dog often becomes more excited and works even faster and more intently, possibly to keep the person from getting away. The dog's handler can generally see this change in behavior and knows when the dog is close to the person. The handler's own behavior might change to reflect this knowledge by calling out to the person to establish voice contact or starting to walk faster to get closer to the dogs. Generally, trailing dog teams work in close enough proximity to one another that the handler remains in visual range of the dog when it makes its discovery, even when the dog works off lead. However, the person may be hidden from sight—which doesn't inhibit the dog, only the handler. In these situations, handlers again rely on the clear communication from the dog to tell them that they're near or that they've found the subject.

Although an air scent dog usually works farther away from the handler than does a trailing dog, the handlers can see when their dog has pinpointed the location of the missing person by the dramatic alert. It's thrilling to see an air scent dog's head and muzzle lift high and watch the dog run deliberately back and forth across the scent cone until it finally runs straight to the missing person as the scent cone narrows to the source of the scent. Even when the person is too far away to be seen, or is hidden from view, most dog handlers have no doubt when their dog is successful. In these situations, an air scent handler usually runs after the dog to get to the missing person as quickly as possible.

Safety and Priorities

There's a maxim in search and rescue: "Your safety comes first, your team members' next, then the safety of the victim." The logic of this may be apparent and is certainly realistic. If anyone helping the victim is injured, they're unable to provide any assistance and even become a liability. In canine search and rescue handlers know that their own safety and that of their dogs is their primary concern. Prioritizing the safety of others over that of their own or their dog's is a mistake. If either become injured or can no longer continue to search, a valuable resource has been lost to others in need.

Trust in the partnership extends to the belief that neither the dog nor the handler will place the other in jeopardy. The atmosphere around search and rescue is exciting and it may be easy for a handler to get caught up in the thrill of the mission and the strong desire to help. Most search dogs will do whatever their handlers ask once the partnership becomes solid, and the handlers must be able to keep their dogs safe in all situations. Other members of a search agency also appreciate handlers who knows how to take care of themselves and their dog. Many emergency service personnel will only work with others who demonstrate an ability to make wise decisions and take care of themselves. As much as search dogs contribute to others, they certainly deserve this assurance in return.

Elements of the partnership between the search dog and the handler described in this chapter develop through living, training, practicing, and working together. This partnership is one in which neither individual can be as effective as the two together when there's respect, trust, and clear communication.

Chapter Nine

Avalanche Rescue

A valanches are snow slides that occur when the supporting layers of snow become weak and suddenly give way, causing the upper layers to collapse and slide down the side of a mountain. Avalanches may be triggered naturally by high winds or temperature variations, or may be caused by humans or animals crossing above or through zones where the snow pack is weak. Most people know what avalanches are, but the effects of the devastation caused are hard to imagine. The snow descends with alarming speed and can even leave debris fields that are over 200 yards wide, and several feet deep, with blocks of compacted snow as large as trucks. The snow sets quickly and has the consistency of cement.

Avalanche Precaution

Avalanches are closely associated with ski resort areas, although ski resort personnel manage any potential avalanches before skiers arrive for the day. Avalanches occur through-

out the world in mountainous terrain where the angles of the slopes are conducive to snow sliding and snow conditions are unstable or changes in weather and temperature contribute to instability. Ski resorts manage avalanche control programs by setting off explosives that cause weak snow to slide, but there can be very little control in the wilderness. The increased popularity of winter sports outside of the bounds of ski resorts, such as snowmobiling, snowshoeing, snowboarding, and backcountry or cross-country skiing, have increased the number of people caught in avalanches in the wilderness.

Finding Victims

Ski patrol and search and rescue personnel are trained to respond quickly to avalanches when there's a possibility that someone is buried. When someone is caught in an avalanche in the wilderness, response time may not be as fast as necessary to save a life. When the victim is buried alive (as opposed to being killed upon impact), the speed of response is critical, as the window of possibility of finding someone alive drops by 30 percent in the first 15 minutes of burial and is reduced to 50 percent after 30 minutes. For this reason, the effectiveness of resources is determined by how quickly and accurately they can pinpoint the location of a buried victim. The most effective resource for pinpointing the location of a victim buried in an avalanche is a trained avalanche search dog.

Although remote, avalanches are frequently responsible for the loss of life. It's becoming more likely that avalanche dogs will be able to save lives in these situations as well. Charley Shimanksi, education director of The Mountain Rescue Association, notes, "The proliferation of cell phones in the backcountry could have a dramatic impact on the search and rescue dog's ability to find survivors in avalanches. Now,

A sign warns skiers of a dangerous avalanche-prone area.

we're often notified by cell phones just minutes after the accident . . . [W]e can get a rescue dog and handler to the scene within a matter of minutes. Someday . . . that will mean the difference between life and death." In Colorado, a state with one of the highest rates of death due to avalanches, a rapid deployment, or avalanche deployment, program has been initiated by Flight for Life, a helicopter medical service, to pick up and deliver trained and certified rescue resources to the sight of an avalanche within minutes.

Dogs specifically trained in avalanche rescue are trained to cover an avalanche debris field quickly to find anyone who may be buried under several feet of snow. It's not unusual to find someone buried in more than ten feet of snow in an avalanche. When someone is buried under the snow, their scent is carried through the porous composition of the snow and eventually rises to the surface. Once it reaches the surface it's carried in the air, where the avalanche dogs use air-scenting techniques to locate the buried victim.

An avalanche dog is trained to find living or dead victims, and even articles buried in the snow, with their priority being a live victim. A trained avalanche dog can locate a buried victim within minutes—the time it takes just to set up a search using beacons or a line of searchers with probe poles. In fact, dogs certified in avalanche rescue are considered part of the hasty, or rapid deployment team, on an avalanche mission.

Flight For Life's rapid response Avalanche Deployment gets dog teams to avalanches quickly.

Ideally, the avalanche dog teams are sent into the *debris field* or *avalanche deposition zone,* while other mission resources are still being coordinated.

The Avalanche Beacon

Avalanche beacons can be effective if the buried victim is wearing a beacon and it's turned on to transmit at the time the victim was buried. An avalanche beacon is a small, battery operated device designed to transmit or receive continuous signals. When the beacon is set to transmit, its signal can be received by another beacon set to receive the signal. When worn and used effectively, they can help pinpoint the location of

a victim buried under the snow. Even so, using a beacon to find someone buried under several feet of snow requires training and practice, especially when there are several hundred square feet to cover. Rescuers also use probe poles, which are metal poles inserted into the snow at various points with the hope of locating buried victims by touching them with the tip of the pole. Because the snow has the consistency of concrete soon after it settles, it's often quite difficult to insert even a metal pole into the snow deep enough to make contact with anything under the snow.

Sadly, very few victims buried by avalanches are found alive. The impact of the snow or the effects of being violently swept down the

An avalanche beacon can be a critical piece of equipment when recreating in the mountains in winter.

scent. The handler and other rescuers immediately race to the spot indicated by the dog to dig as well, using shovels to free the victim. The dog handler also uses wands with labeled flagging to mark areas of the dog's alerts so they can continue to search while other search personnel dig at the marked sites. People who are caught in avalanches are frequently buried several feet down, so the rescuers must work quickly and diligently to break through the hard packed snow. Either the first dog continues to help by being brought back to the spot to continue to dig in the direction of the buried victim, or a second dog is brought to the alert area for confirmation.

The location of the strongest scent of the victim may not be directly over the burial. Just as the air above the snow carries scent, air currents also carry scent throughout the snow and around frozen blocks of snow within the debris. The dynamics of scent apply in snow as well as on dry ground. Because the ground and a person's body temperature are warmer than the temperature of snow, the warmer air lifts the scent with it as it travels toward the surface. As the scent rises, air currents may carry it down the slope through the snow or, following the path of least resistance, it may travel around large slabs of snow before rising to the surface. An avalanche dog handler needs to understand scent dynamics and the effects that temperature gradient has on scent in snow.

mountainside and/or hitting rocks and trees often kill them before they are completely buried. If alive when buried, the snow may fill the airway of a victim; if not, the victim may suffocate while buried. The best chance of surviving an avalanche is, quite simply, not to get caught in one.

Going Into Action

When an avalanche dog and handler arrive on scene, the handler sends the dog into the debris field using hand signals or a *directed send.* The handler often continues to signal direction changes for the dog from a distance, always moving the dog into the wind. When the dog alerts to the source of the scent from a buried victim, it begins to dig and often bark as the means of alerting to the location of the source of the

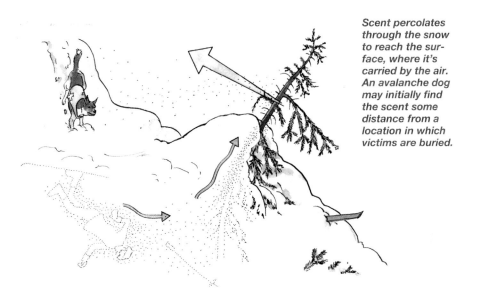

Scent percolates through the snow to reach the surface, where it's carried by the air. An avalanche dog may initially find the scent some distance from a location in which victims are buried.

Training the Avalanche Dog

Basic training starts with air scent runaway problems (described in Chapter Six, Air Scent) in the snow. With a helper holding the dog, the dog's handler encourages the dog as she runs away into the wind and jumps into a snow pit. The objective is to imprint the search command while playing the hide-and-seek game that search dogs love so much. When the dog gets to the handler in the snow pit, it's encouraged to jump in with the handler and play with the toy or a glove as a reward. When the dog understands the game, which happens quickly, the visual cues are removed—as they are in training a wilderness search dog. Continuing to use the

snow pit as the handler's end point, the handler is covered with a light dusting of snow. At this point, the dog also begins its formal training to find scent through snow. As the dog progresses in training and performs well, the handler stays with the dog while another person hides.

Training the dog to work out more complex problems is accomplished by burying willing subjects in snow pits or caves. The snow caves are dug several feet into the snow and covered with blocks of snow of various depths and consistencies. When the dog finds the buried subject's scent, it's encouraged to dig through the blocks of snow and even climb into the snow cave to get to the subject to play with its toy reward, which is held by the subject. The dog is encouraged to pull on the toy as

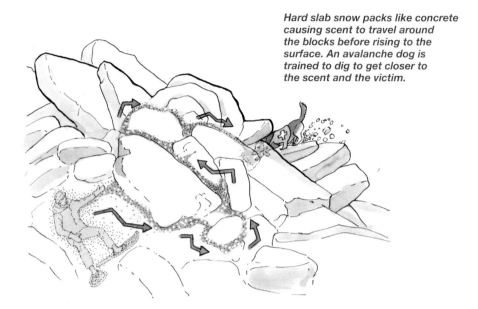

Hard slab snow packs like concrete causing scent to travel around the blocks before rising to the surface. An avalanche dog is trained to dig to get closer to the scent and the victim.

well, increasing its determination and sometimes literally pulling the subject out of the snow cave. Some dogs bark as well as dig to alert the handler to their find.

Avalanche Dogs at Work

Many ski resorts now employ avalanche dogs on site to work on the ski slopes. The avalanche dogs report to work every day and are stationed on the mountainside with other ski patrol personnel. They ride the chair lifts to the top of the ski runs each day to be ready for rapid deployment to any spot on the mountain or to the landing zone for the quick helicopter flight to an avalanche. They're also trained to ride in snowmobiles and sleds in order to move around the mountain quickly. Avalanche rescue dog handlers must enjoy spending long hours in snow and enjoy skiing. They should also be able to drive a snowmobile or at least ride on one with their dog sitting in front of them or across their lap. Avalanche dog handlers need to become well educated in the mechanics of avalanches, winter weather patterns, snow travel, wilderness winter survival, and avalanche safety, in addition to the theoretical, practical, and operational requirements of certifying as an avalanche rescue dog team.

A job at a ski resort requires that an avalanche dog have a tremendous amount of social interaction with strangers and large crowds of skiers, so it must enjoy people in order to

An avalanche dog and its support have located a buried victim.

work at a ski resort. All avalanche dogs must be able to tolerate cold temperatures and be able to move comfortably through snow. Of course, an avalanche dog team must live in an area where avalanches are prevalent and their services are needed. They need to be able to get to the avalanche as quickly as possible.

In her book *Avalanche! Hasty Search, The Training and Care of Avalanche Search and Rescue Dogs,* (Doral Publishing, 2003), Patti Burnett describes the love, care, and dedication that goes into training avalanche rescue dogs and being part of avalanche rescue operations. The book specifically describes the progression of training and provides descriptions of avalanche training exercises. Burnett also describes some of the many avalanches she and her dogs, Hasty and Sandy, have responded to, along with other avalanche dog handlers and rescue personnel.

Chapter Ten
Water Search

People drown under a wide range of circumstances. They may be fishing from a boat on a lake, white water rafting on a river, or just wading along the banks of a fast-moving creek or stream. When a drowning occurs and witnesses are unable to retrieve the person safely, various resources are called on to help recover the victim. Typical resources used to locate a drowned victim include sonar devices and divers. Sonar devices show shapes under water, but can't always determine whether the image on the screen is that of a human. Divers always go into the water to recover a body, but it's often difficult to see underwater, especially in lakes that are murky. Rivers can pose a threat to safety, even to trained divers, due to their fast currents in combination with rocks and other obstacles.

Timing Is Crucial

Water search is a term used to describe the process of locating victims of drowning, either in lakes or rivers. The length of time victims of a drowning are submerged and the temperature of the water may contribute to their ability to survive. In a cold-water drowning, a person may still be resuscitated after having been submerged for up to an hour. Because time is a factor in survivability, immediately locating the victim is critical. Search personnel respond quickly to determine the victim's location in order to save a life. However, most frequently the chances of survival are minimal due to the circumstances, so in these cases the speed of discovery is less critical than it is following an avalanche—although it is still important. Rapid response and deployment are always initiated in cases of drowning and, with increasing frequency, dogs are an integral part of this response.

How Dogs Find Drowning Victims

Dogs trained to find people in water have been extremely effective in finding the scent of drowned victims after the scent, in the form of vapors and gases, rises to the surface of the

Swift water searches can pose a threat to a dog team's safety.

water. Water search dogs use air-scenting techniques to determine the location of the strongest scent in a body of water or to narrow the search area for divers, who may then go into the water to find and recover the body of the victim.

Several factors influence the ability of a water search dog team to determine the location of a victim. Water currents carry the scent of a drowned victim, which is subsequently moved by the air when it exits the water, just as it is when the scent source is on land or in snow. Depending on the wind, the depth of the water, the speed of the currents, and the size of the body of water, water search dogs can often find the scent from the shore. Other factors that influence how scent behaves in water are the

thermoclines, or the temperature differences in the water. There may be multiple layers of different water temperatures, so it's possible for the scent to rise in warmer water, only to hit colder water and move along with the current some distance before rising again when it hits warmer temperatures. Scent may also catch in weeds and between rocks or anything in the water before surfacing, as it does on land.

The physiology of a drowned body can also determine where a water search dog finds scent. As the body fills with gases, it rises with warmer temperatures. A body may also be affected by thermoclines when it comes into contact with a level of colder water, where it can remain suspended until the temperatures

Thermoclines effect how a drowning victim's scent travels through water and where it surfaces.

rise. As a drowned body decomposes, the skin may slip off and move into another area of the water, causing search dogs to alert on the skin or tissue.

Searching Techniques

When searching a body of still water or a lake, water search dogs often search along the shoreline and from boats. Always working with the wind blowing toward them, search dog teams walk along the shore of a lake, often as a preliminary step to determine if the dog can narrow an area of a large lake in which to work. When working from boats, water search dogs and handlers work grid patterns in an attempt to find the scent, exactly as they would in a wilderness search. When searching from a boat, a water search dog team asks a helper to navigate the boat by moving it in a grid pattern, tacking back and forth into the wind, while following the dog's alerts. When the dog alerts to the strongest scent and the boat is moved into position directly over the scent, the handler analyzes where the scent is coming from by calculating the strength of current and wind. Search dog handlers drop buoys to mark areas of their dogs' alerts in a lake. These buoys serve to triangulate the dogs' alerts and narrow the search area for the divers to search. Rescue

Dogs often search from boats.

divers can then follow up by searching the area of alerts underwater and recover the person.

Dogs are also valuable in narrowing the range of the search area for victims who have drowned in rivers or other moving water. When a drowning has occurred in a river, especially where there's fastmoving water (referred to as *white water* or *swift water*), dogs search from the shore. It's also possible for a dog to search from a boat in moving water if the river is large enough that the boat can be safely navigated. Due to the behavior of scent in moving water, it's possible for a search dog to alert to scent several miles downstream from where the body is actually submerged in the water. The scent is carried in the moving water and may be pushed down below the surface for a few miles before surfacing. If the body has

begun to decompose, tissue is most likely torn off by the movement of the currents and by fish, and is carried farther downstream. The body may even become lodged beneath a rock or log, where it continues to emit scent. In a river search, the search dog teams begin to search downstream from where the victim was known to have gone into the water. The team's objective is to have the dogs search as they work upstream and into the wind. When a boat is used in moving water, the navigator steers the boat back and forth between the banks as the handler watches the dog for an alert in a specific area. If the dog alerts in a specific area in a swift water search, the handler marks the point of the alert and the wind direction at the time of the alert on a map and/or marks the point on the shoreline for divers to return.

A dog searches along the banks of a river.

Search Dog Body Language

Search dogs exhibit a variety of reactions when they alert to scent from the water, so the handlers each look for their own dog's particular style of alert. Some dogs may bite the water in order to taste the scent, others bark in the direction of the scent, or may even attempt to jump into the water. It's important to prevent the dog from jumping into the water from a boat or from the shore, especially when the river is moving swiftly. A search dog will typically try to get closer to the scent in any search situation, but for its own safety it should be restrained in water searches.

Some dogs show interest from a distance and the boat can be steered in the direction the dog's nose points when the dog first alerts

to scent. As the boat is steered in the direction of the alert, those on shore often see a beautifully defined grid pattern as the boat follows the direction the dog's nose points. When the dog finds the edges of the scent cone, its head turns and so should the boat. The distance between the boat's tacks back and forth across the cone narrows as the boat approaches the source of the scent.

A water search dog needs to be very comfortable riding in a boat and should initially be introduced to the boat on land, where it can get in and practice sitting quietly before sitting in the boat in the water. Once comfortable in the boat on land, the dog should be taught to step into the boat and ride quietly on the water. It's important for the dog to feel stable while riding in a boat, so it will concentrate on the lessons and its job

A dog should first become comfortable in a boat in dock before going out into a lake.

rather than worrying about the new sensations. Many search dogs wear their harness and/or a life vest made for dogs when searching from boats. The dog should become familiar with the harness or life vest before actual water search training starts.

Training the Water Search Dog

Search dogs usually begin water search training from the shore of a lake, where the dogs and handlers can become comfortable working in and around bodies of water. The initial objective is to introduce the idea of human scent in water to the dog. To do this, the basic runaway is

again used, only this time the runaway is into the water. The subject, often a diver, uses a toy and plays with the dog on the shore at the edge of a lake with the wind blowing toward him from across the lake. Then, stepping into the lake, the subject encourages the dog to follow, staying at a depth where the dog can comfortably wade and play with the subject or receive food treats from the subject in the water. This game should continue until the dog is completely comfortable with being in and around water.

As the dog's comfort level progresses, the diver can move farther into the lake while the dog watches. Once the diver is in the lake and submerged, the dog gets into the boat and begins the search pattern into the wind, toward the diver. At this point, the visual connection with the diver no longer exists, so the diver is lost to the dog. It's important for the handler to stay focused on the dog and watch for an alert and any changes in the dog's behavior that show the dog has identified the scent emanating from the water. The helper steers the boat in response to the dog's alerts until the dog's nose is very near the scent source, in the same way a dog on land would work itself into a scent cone. The submerged diver should come to the surface of the water and present the food reward or toy reward to the dog and play while the dog receives lots of praise. It's important to have a clear signal to inform the diver when to ascend and reward the dog.

Good timing is a valuable ingredient in helping the dog realize the rewards of water search. The dogs enjoy finding divers when they are able to interact with them as part of their reward, whereas actual searches are limited to the dog finding only the scent.

Once the dog understands its job is to find human scent rising out of the water, it can be introduced to the idea that the scent coming from the body of water can also be detected from the shore. A subject can be enlisted to hide in grasses in the lake, either with her head above water or using a snorkel to drop below the surface of the water. The dog is given the search command and walked along the shoreline into the wind. When the dog alerts to the subject in the water, the subject comes toward the dog to play as the dog is rewarded with praise.

Water search dogs are also trained with the aid of human cadaver scent in the form of hair, teeth, or nails enclosed in a mesh bag or nylon stocking. The scent must escape from the container. These items are anchored off shore at varying distances and the dogs search along the shoreline. When the dogs show interest they may even be encouraged to swim to the item if it's anchored at a safe distance in safe water. Dogs usually act excited when they recognize human scent in the water, even when it's in the form of hair or teeth. Some search teams also use a device called a *scent generator* to blow the scent of human tissue up through the water. Either gauze with human scent or tissue is placed in the compartment of the device, and the generator is placed in the water. Air is mechanically pumped through the compartment, causing bubbles to carry the scent to the surface of the water.

Potential Complications

Swift water training is more difficult to set up due to the dangerous nature of the water. Dogs with experience in lakes usually make the transition to swift water smoothly. The key component appears to be human scent rising out of water, whether moving or still. Handlers,

Swift water creates complex scent problems.

however, need to be able to learn about water currents and their effect on scent so that they can read their dogs effectively when working along rivers where the surface scent may be miles away from the source. Victims who have drowned in swift water may be carried downstream or may be caught under rocks or logs. Even though the victim's body is caught in one area, the scent can move throughout the water and be dispersed and spread, as explained in still water scenarios. Scent may be carried downstream for miles before rising to the surface, so the point at which a search dog alerts to a scent may be some distance from the source of the scent.

Complicating matters further, when a body has been immersed for a period of time and tissue is sloughed off, it is carried downstream, carried along branches of the river or stream, and snagged by tree branches or rocks. This creates another scent source that the dog could identify in a separate location. The scent from the body is greater than scent from tissue, but the question for the handler in a swift-water search is, where is the body as compared to the scent?

Chapter Eleven
Disaster Search

The meaning of disaster and the ensuing searches are vivid in the minds of most people today. Whether the disaster is the result of a phenomenon of nature or caused by man, the effects are tragic and devastating. Disasters include earthquakes, tornadoes, floods, hurricanes, explosions, and airline crashes. Governments and local agencies work together to coordinate the resources trained to respond to disasters throughout the world. In the United States, the Federal Emergency Management Agency (FEMA) has developed educational programs, standards and certification programs to provide technical assistance when disasters occur. When the disaster affects people, these national resources may be requested through local, state, and national agencies and are deployed very quickly. Their objective is to rescue survivors who might be buried in structures and/or mud and debris. People around the world watch as the horrific effects of disasters unfold on television. The incomprehensible devastation of the bombing in Oklahoma City and the attacks on the Pentagon and the World Trade Center has brought the reality home to Americans. Responses to disasters of this magnitude require technical expertise.

Urban Disaster

The Urban Search and Rescue (US&R) program was developed by FEMA in 1990 to provide highly qualified technical assistance to local agencies responding to major disasters. FEMA provides assistance through task forces or search teams organized to respond with specialists in the areas of hazardous materials, structural, technical search, and canine search. The teams are certified through the FEMA certification program. FEMA has been instrumental in developing standards and techniques, and in training and certifying personnel deployed in response to the disasters in Oklahoma City, Washington D.C., New York City, Pennsylvania, and Texas following the crash of the space shuttle *Columbia,* as well as natural disasters, such as hurricanes in Florida and North Carolina and earthquakes in California.

Disaster sites are dangerous and need special considerations before searching.

It's important to have several types of specialists available and working together at disaster sites. The areas must be made relatively safe before searchers can move in to search, so the site may need to be cleared of hazardous material or other dangerous influences. It's also necessary to physically shore up the precarious structures before they can be entered and walked across or through. Tools available to search for buried people are seismic listening devices, heat seeking devices, and cameras. This technology can be helpful when the space or area being viewed is accessible to humans and their tools. In spite of the impressive technology, cameras are most effec-tive when used in association with trained search dogs.

How Disaster Response Dogs Work

Disaster response dogs are trained to find scent and point the technicians to the most likely location of its source. For example, as minute amounts of scent escape through cracks that are too narrow to see into, fiber optic cameras can be lowered to verify the dog's discovery. Sometimes the fiber winds down through several levels and around corners before revealing the victim. The fact that the

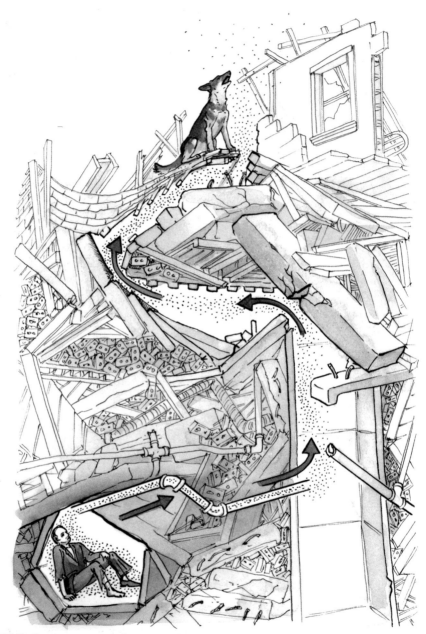

FEMA disaster response dogs are trained to find live victims and bark to indicate the scent as it travels up through a maze of rubble, pipes, and often hazardous fumes and solid materials.

victim's scent must first move around and through these obstacles, yet is still detected by dogs, reinforces the dogs' remarkable capabilities.

Using air scenting techniques, disaster response dogs search among rubble from collapsed structures, and other debris to pinpoint the location where the highest concentration of scent escapes from a person who is trapped or buried. The dynamics of scent are somewhat similar to those found in avalanche rescue with slab avalanches and in water rescue, in which the location where human scent reaches the surface of the snow or water may be some distance from where a person is buried or drowned. The difference in the scent for dogs responding to a disaster is the level of complexity of the problems, due to pipes, culverts, and the way air channels scent through shafts and tunnels created after a structure collapses. Determining the exact location of the source of scent can also be challenging after a disaster because of the influence dust and chemicals have on the dog's nose and the way scent moves in these chaotic and confusing environments.

The position of FEMA canine search specialist was created as a critical component of each FEMA task force. The training and certification program was designed to ensure the accuracy and safety of each search dog team in the program, whether responding to domestic or international situations. In order to be certified, each dog and handler team must pass an intense national certification in urban search and rescue.

The number of dogs deployed to search at the World Trade Center was the largest in the history of this country. Approximately 80 FEMA dog teams were used to search following the attack at the World Trade Center and approximately 20 FEMA dog teams were deployed at the Pentagon. The fact that no FEMA-certified disaster response dog or handler was killed while searching at the Pentagon or the World Trade Center, and the only physical injuries sustained by the dogs certified under FEMA were cuts and abrasions, is a testament to the effectiveness of the program.

Each dog team works in 12-hour shifts to search a disaster site or areas within the site. The dog teams are given breaks of 20 to 45 minutes between similar working periods. The dogs are trained to be able to work out of the handler's sight, although the handler remains as close as physically possible. As is true with all search and rescue dog handlers, they are responsible for ensuring that their dog remains safe. FEMA-certified disaster response dogs are trained to find live human scent coming from underneath the rubble. Once found, the dogs are trained to stay at the spot and bark for as long as necessary to alert the handler to their discovery.

In order to reach many of the areas that the dogs must work, they are trained to follow their handlers' signals, or follow the *directed send*. The directed send is used to move a dog into a rubble pile and to send

Disaster response dogs are encouraged to play tug as their reward for finding the victim.

the dog into another area of the rubble when the handler is too far from the dog to be audible. This means that among the extreme noise and confusion at disaster sites, the dog must concentrate and focus only on its job and its handler's signals.

The dogs are trained to respond immediately to voice commands as well, whether or not they can see their handler. The commands used to guide the dog, such as "up," "climb," "down," "crawl," and "off," are also a critical component of training in order to keep the dog safe while working. Commands such as "slow," "steady," "back," "wait," and "stop" may mean the difference between life and death for the dog and others on the site. The dangers at Ground Zero in New York City were constant. One of the dogs working a distance from its handler detected scent from a hole and ran toward it to investigate further, with the intention of entering the hole to get closer to the scent source. Upon seeing the hole, the handler yelled "stop!" and got an immediate response from the dog. When the handler got to the hole and looked into it to determine the level of risk, she saw that it dropped straight down for at least 75 feet.

Special Skills

Search dogs must stay calm in any transport, such as a litter that may be pulled across a chasm. The dogs are also trained to wait for assistance in navigating particularly difficult movements and to rappel when necessary. The ability to crawl into tight spaces is also required. Handlers may need to go through a small opening into a narrow space and have someone else hand the dog in to him. For this reason, the dog must be willing to let other people handle it. A FEMA disaster response dog may not display any signs of aggression when working very closely with other dogs and people.

The disaster response dog team works hard to develop precision in timing and response to commands. Even when the dog works at some distance from the handler, which is the norm in disaster search, the handler watches the dog and the area closely for any danger to the dog. Precise timing is often crucial, along with the handler's ability to perceive the dog's next move and the condition of the debris where the dog works. This ability is often necessary in order to stop the dog from any motion that could destabilize an already precarious area, before an accident happens.

FEMA Standards

Many local search and rescue dog teams have also adopted the standards developed by FEMA, although there are also disaster response dogs trained under other local standards. All disaster response dogs must meet the rigorous requirements determined by the environment in which they work. The FEMA model is described here.

There are two levels of certification for a FEMA canine search specialist or disaster response dog team: Type II and Type I. The basic classification is Type II. These dog teams are required to pass tests showing non-aggression, obedience, agility, the bark alert, and the bark alert on a rubble pile while out of sight. Type I is the advanced classification, where the dog has passed the basic tests and is also able to locate and alert to six victims who are buried in three separate rubble piles that have also been contaminated with food, clothing, and distractions from other animals.

The dogs are trained in five elements, developed specifically to prepare a dog to search disaster sites independently and effectively with confidence while staying safe. The five elements are obedience and control, agility, the directed send, the bark/live find indication, and the rubble search.

The importance of clean and clear obedience has already been discussed. Obedience and control are integral aspects of all other elements of disaster work. Basic obedience, including heeling on and off leash, sit and down-stays, and recall, can be trained in various settings. Commands are both verbal and with hand signals. The commands and signals used to control the dog include "wait," "stop," "easy," "turn around," "back," and "stay." These commands should be used while training for agility as well as being introduced separately. As with all other training, obedience and control commands should be fun for the handler and the dog.

Agility training has been described by Ann Wichmann, Type I canine search specialist for the FEMA Colorado Task Force, as "giving our dogs four-wheel drive." The objective of training for agility is to learn how to carefully maneuver through difficult situations. Disaster response dogs must be able to balance and walk along high, narrow, teetering boards and climb ladders that are set at an angle of 45 degrees, as well as shift their weight when unstable surfaces move. The dogs must also be able to crawl through tight spaces and along tunnels, as well as stop and back out of an area without moving from side to side. Commands are used to guide the dog along the course, which makes it a great environment for the dog to learn, practice, and perfect what it will use on actual missions.

Obstacle courses set up by teams and/or handlers are built to train and perfect search dogs' agility capabilities. These courses should be dynamic so that they can be modified to prepare the dog to accept new circumstances and face strange situations. The courses have been referred to as "extreme agility" and include any type of obstacle the handler believes the dog will encounter in extreme situations. The dogs are trained with patience and encouragement so that they can not only feel comfortable, but will have fun playing on the course and meeting each new challenge.

Another element is the *directed send*. The purpose of the directed send is to send the dog into the rubble from a distance, then have it move in various directions. The dog must learn to watch the handler and wait for the next hand signal. FEMA tests the directed send by setting up a course in a baseball diamond pattern where the handler directs the dog to each obstacle, often a platform or a pallet. The dog is directed to jump up on the platform, where it must remain for five seconds, in response to the handler's signal.

Training for the directed send also combines play with obedience and control. As with other elements, this is introduced as a game that becomes more difficult only after the dog masters each stage. The first stage is to teach the dog to jump up on the pallet or platform on command. Gradually, the handler and dog move back from the pallet and the command to jump up on the pallet is combined with the send portion of the element. The dog needs to learn to move forward, back, on it, wait, left, and right in order to move to each station in the baseball diamond on the directed send.

The next element, the bark alert/live find indication, is something that can be difficult, even impossible, for some dogs. They must first be willing to bark on command in order to learn to bark as their alert. They must also bark continuously for a minimum of 30 seconds to notify the handler that a person they can't see is in a space they can't see. Some dogs simply aren't able to sustain the bark alert. Wichmann finds that a disaster response dog needs to have a very concentrated focus. It's not unusual to see a dog trained exclusively in disaster work locate scent in

Disaster response dogs are trained to find human scent in piles of concrete rubble.

the rubble pile and start the bark alert as soon as it gets scent. What's missing from these dogs is the ability to continue working until they locate the most concentrated area of scent, or the source of scent. Cross-training the dogs in wilderness search seems to give the dogs the ability to continue working after they initially find the scent, until they pinpoint the source of the scent before barking.

The dogs are encouraged to focus on toys as rewards in training, so that they can receive their rewards immediately when they find the victim and bark for the prescribed length of time. Play and praise are used to keep up the dog's motivation on a sustained bark and all other aspects of disaster search.

Training begins with a runaway problem, as it does with other search techniques, but with disaster dogs the runaway is into a barrel, called a *bark barrel.* The handler is the dog's first subject and encourages the dog with a tug toy as a helper holds the dog. The handler then runs and crawls into a barrel as she teases the dog with the toy. Once the dog is released, the handler keeps the toy hidden so the dog has to bark first to receive the reward. As soon as the dog barks and tries to get the toy, the handler rewards the dog by immediately praising and playing with the dog, offering to tug back and forth with the toy.

As the dog becomes more confident with the objective of barking to get the toy, the door of the bark barrel can be used to cover the opening so the dog can no longer see the toy. The door has holes drilled in it so scent can escape through the cover. Once the dog works confidently while barking at the handler, another person hides in the barrel. Once the dog accomplishes this stage with a strong, confident bark, the visual cue can be removed.

The helper hides in the barrel and covers the opening before the dog enters the area. The handler moves the dog into place 25 yards from the barrel and releases the dog with the search command. When the dog barks for the pre-defined length of time or number of barks, the door is opened and the helper plays with the dog vigorously. Eventually, as the dog's *live find bark* is strong and consistent, other barrels can be added to the problem so the dog doesn't associate barking with the sight of any barrel. The subject hides in only one of the barrels out of the dog's sight, and the dog is then sent to find the subject and bark. This also prepares the dog to search for live human scent in the rubble pile.

The previous four elements come together in the final element, the rubble search. The dog must be willing to be directed into the rubble pile and navigate through its complexities to find human scent. Once the dog locates the strongest scent, it's

required to stay at the spot and bark continuously until released. The American Rescue Dog Association (ARDA) recommends not starting a dog on the rubble pile until it is steady and consistent in the other four elements, as described in their book, *Search and Rescue Dogs, Training the K-9 Hero.* The dog's focus needs to be intense enough to search on the rubble pile without losing confidence. It must continue to bark while its handler approaches and until released. ARDA suggests placing the bark barrel on the rubble pile the first time the dog is introduced to searching and finding someone hidden in the pile. Eventually, subjects are hidden in different holes in the rubble. The dog is sent into the rubble from different angles, giving it the opportunity to work through various problems to find and get to the scent. The bark alert continues to be reinforced through play in the rubble pile.

Disaster work is very specialized and requires focused commitment from the handler and the dog. This focus must be intense and the dog's motivation kept high with the reward of play and praise. As with all search and rescue disciplines, the experiences should be made fun and positive during training. To learn about FEMA's requirements and testing procedures, visit their web site, *www.FEMA.org.*

Chapter Twelve
Cadaver Dogs

With the exception of FEMA disaster response dogs trained to find live victims, search dogs are expected to locate missing individuals, whether living or dead. Wilderness dogs are expected to find and alert on bodies, although they are not necessarily trained specifically on cadaver scent. Cadaver dogs are trained to locate recently deceased or decomposing bodies, tissue, bones, fluid, or body parts. They are frequently used in law enforcement situations to locate victims of crime and human remains as forensic evidence. As with other search techniques, the dogs search for scent emanating from the cadaver material, no matter where it's found. Cadaver dogs are trained to look for scent above and below the ground and among extreme contamination such as that found in landfills or garbage dumps.

Highly Specialized Skills

Human remains detection refers to dogs trained to find fresh or decomposing human remains. All dogs trained in wilderness, avalanche, and water search would be included in this broad category. *Cadaver search dogs* are becoming more specialized within their classification and may be separated into unique categories. One category is the cadaver search dog trained to alert on the scent source of human tissue, blood, other body fluids, and materials that have been handled and worn by humans. These dogs are often cross-trained for other purposes in search and rescue. Another is the *forensic search dog,* which is specifically trained to alert to a scent source from decomposing human tissue and not alert to scent from human body fluids or residual scent from a live human. The forensic search dog is trained specifically for evidence gathering in law enforcement situations.

Cadaver dogs use air-scenting techniques to alert to and locate human remains. Although many dogs trained in cadaver are also cross-trained in wilderness search, the cadaver dogs are specifically trained to use different search techniques when searching for decomposed cadavers. Although they are air scenting, instead of working far ahead of the handlers, cadaver dogs are trained to work near handlers while executing close grid searches and working meticulously with their noses near the ground to locate very minute traces of scent.

Training the Cadaver Dog

When dogs already trained for wilderness search begin cadaver training, their handlers use a search command that's different from the command used to search for missing people in a wilderness search. Cadaver dogs are also trained to respond with various indications to alert the handler to the scent source. The alerts could be active indications, such as barking or scratching. They may also be trained to use passive indications, such as sitting or lying down, when they find the scent source. If they're being trained to respond to disasters, cadaver dogs should not dig for their alert, given the instability of the environment following a disaster. When minute amounts of tissue or body fluids are identified, dogs may also turn or lift their head in the direction of the remains, so the handler must remain sensitive to the dog's behavior.

Training begins with material from a cadaver, such as bones or teeth, which can be introduced in a container with holes drilled in it to let scent escape. A good container to use when beginning training is a PVC pipe. The pipe can also be used as a toy to create excitement for the dog when it's thrown and even retrieved in the beginning stages of training. Of course, once trained, a cadaver dog doesn't disturb the remains at the site, so retrieving the object is discontinued early in training.

Initially, the pipe containing the cadaver material is shown to the dog as a toy to get the dog excited about playing the new game. It's then thrown into the brush and the dog is taken into the area to find the pipe containing the cadaver material. Susan Bulanda recommends that the handler "carefully note how your dog reacts" during the early stages of cadaver training, in her book *Ready! The Training of the Search and Rescue Dog* (Doral Publishing, 1995). The dog should be encouraged to respond with the preferred alert when it approaches the cadaver material.

The technique of locating buried remains is taught gradually using small amounts of dirt at first as a dusting to cover the enclosed material. The material is progressively covered with more dirt. When the dog understands that what it's looking for may be covered with dirt, it's important to introduce other options. Because the dog needs to focus on scent from cadaver material rather than live human scent, training should include digging other holes and covering them with fresh dirt when digging a hole for the cadaver material. The holes should be allowed to air out for a period of time so that residual scent from the per-

Cadaver dogs air scent in tight patterns close to the ground to find buried cadaver material and fluids.

son who dug the hole can blow away. The dog is then encouraged to ignore the living human's scent and look for the scent from the cadaver material. This training can continue until the dog finds remains buried at the depth of a shallow grave.

Various objects are also used to hide the cadaver material and create choices for the dog. Cement blocks or boxes may be lined up or scattered in an area, requiring the dog to search all the objects to find the one containing the remains. In this way the dog is encouraged to search intently for the source of the scent, building on both prey and hunt drives.

If the dog's alert is to dig at the site of the scent source, a scratch box, in which the cadaver material is hidden, can be used. The dog is given the command to locate the scent source

and runs to the closed or partially open box. The objective is to have the dog scratch at the box, which has its opening built on an angle, to show the handler the source of the scent. If the dog hesitates to scratch readily, a helper can open the box slightly and quickly to reveal more scent while the dog is encouraged to dig.

Cadaver dogs that are sent into disaster sites are trained to work safely in rubble piles and meet the same requirements as disaster response dogs looking for live scent.

Developing Motivation

As with any other search and rescue dog program, training a dog to find human remains should be a posi-

A cadaver dog locates the scent of human remains in a cabin.

tive experience for the dog and the handler. The dog receives its reward and praise based on its accomplishment. Training is aimed at keeping the dog's motivation high and its experiences successful. Bulanda refers to the fact that some dogs have been reported to show an aversion to cadaver work and may even begin to work without enthusiasm. Whether the dog is sensing the handler's emotional reaction to the nature of the search or the dog's response is solely its own, it may be necessary to mix cadaver training with training on live victims to maintain high motivation.

At the Pentagon and the World Trade Center, the disaster response dog handlers reported interesting reactions from their dogs, when they compared notes. The dogs trained to indicate live victims frequently indicated cadaver scent, yet continued to search for the live victims as they were trained. The dogs trained on cadaver scent worked constantly as well, alerting on the cadaver, which became overwhelming to some since they were constantly alerting throughout each shift. It appeared to be more challenging for the cadaver dogs to work among the horrendous circumstances because there was so much source scent to alert to throughout the search.

Cadaver Dog Handbook: Forensic Training and Tactics for the Recovery of Human Remains by Andrew J. Rebmann (CRC Press, 2000) is an excellent source for learning more about cadaver search and the training of cadaver dogs.

Chapter Thirteen

Search and Rescue Agencies

Joining a search and rescue agency is highly recommended when one exists in the local area. Search and rescue units are usually associated with a local sheriff's office in the western United States, and may respond within a specific county or be available statewide. Search and rescue units specializing in search dog training, certification, and resources usually respond throughout the state or region with which they're associated. They generally exist independent from other non-canine-based search agencies, although they are available to provide certified dog teams for missions in conjunction with the other search units' technical response. In fact, many dog team handlers also belong to other search and rescue agencies. Examples of this are California Rescue Dog Association (CARDA) and Search and Rescue Dogs of Colorado (SARDOC), two of the older and larger search dog organizations in the western United States.

On the East Coast and in the Midwest it's rare for a search and rescue agency to be associated with law enforcement. Instead, they are inde-pendent entities that are more closely associated with emergency services agencies, although they may be dispatched through a law enforcement resource. Mid-Atlantic Search Dogs, a well-established group that responds to missions in Maryland, Virginia, and Delaware, is one example. Some search and rescue agencies in the eastern United States also combine their technical rescue resources with the training and deployment of their member dog teams.

Team Advantage

A search dog team provides the type of support that is hard to find through any other source. These teams have specific standards for training and certification so they can provide the most consistent support possible on missions. Established training programs are necessary to prepare the novice dog and handler for the rigors of working a search dog effectively on actual search missions.

Working one-on-one with other search dog handlers is also valuable.

They can offer advice and support for each level of training the dog and for becoming a knowledgeable search dog handler. No one can provide the kind of first-hand information about mission protocol for search dogs, specific areas in the wilderness, and particular search experiences as can other search dog handlers.

How Agencies Help Search Teams

Because training requires very specialized situations and resources, it's often difficult to find what's needed to train a search dog well and frequently unless there is support from fellow team members. Search and rescue agencies and

A search dog ignores animal cadavers while searching for human scent.

search dog teams work together to provide the best resources to complete each search mission successfully. Search dog agencies can also educate search and rescue ground personnel (as opposed to dog handlers) and those trained in technical rescue. Members of search and rescue agencies that specialize in other aspects of mission response can also educate dog handlers about mission requirements and protocols—knowledge that is necessary, but isn't generally learned in conjunction with training a search dog.

Finally, working with a search and rescue agency increases a dog team's chance of being deployed on missions quickly. Because calls for assistance are made through official channels, a certified dog team must be included in the list of available resources for that agency. In many states, there are search and rescue boards that include representatives from the search teams in the community. The board members work together to stay informed about current issues and concerns, and may even provide a platform for sharing information. Statewide search and rescue boards are also contacted when there's a need for search dog teams to respond locally and nationwide. The National Association of Search and Rescue (NASAR) has a list of search and rescue agencies throughout the United States, which can be found on the Internet at *www.NASAR.org.*

A trailing dog's nose is kept moist.

Preparing search dogs for a mission.

Chapter Fourteen
Search Missions

Following are descriptions of a few of the many search and rescue missions that occur throughout the United States. The missions were chosen as examples of the broad range of emergencies search and rescue dog teams respond to regularly. No individual mission is indicative of all missions, because each situation and the surrounding circumstances are different from one mission to the next. Dog handlers with many years of experience often say that they can never guess the outcome of any mission.

Sugar Factory Explosion— Disaster

Situation

An explosion blew up a sugar plant in Nebraska, destroying the whole plant, including the silos. The explosion occurred on Saturday and one person was still missing when the disaster response dog teams were called.

Response Teams

Two disaster response dog teams were called in from Colorado to search for the missing worker on Tuesday.

Search Area

Tons of concrete, sugar, and dead, sugar-coated pigeons that had been roosting in the silos before the explosion were everywhere. The dead pigeons added contamination to the scent through which the dogs had to work. In addition to the devastation above ground, there were underground storage areas with shafts that created several channels under the silos that could carry the scent along underground pathways before it reached the surface. There was also three inches of molasses in some of the search areas.

Search Description

Upon arrival at the site, one of the FEMA-certified disaster response dogs, a black Labrador Retriever, initially showed interest in what appeared to be scent from a silo that was collapsed, but still leaning precariously. The safety technician refused to allow the dog team access to the silo for fear of its complete collapse, even though the dog continued to show interest in scent from the area.

The dog teams worked other areas in the site, until the silo could be secured. While the dogs worked through the collapsed structures and moved to the shafts, one of the dogs was suddenly caught up in an avalanche of sugar, carrying the search dog down a shaft. A much worse situation was prevented when the handler saw the sugar avalanche and, with a single command from a distance, told the dog "stop" so it stopped struggling and rode the sugar slide down the shaft without being buried.

Outcome

At the end of the day the first Lab's handler moved her dog around to the back of the still-leaning silo and, using a directed send, sent the dog into the area from 150 yards away. The dog ran into the silo search area quickly, excited to finally get closer to the scent it had picked up initially when he arrived at the site. The dog sped into the area so quickly that it actually passed the scent, flipped around and moved back to the location where the scent was strongest, indicating that the victim was dead. (If the victim had still been alive, the alert would have been a strong, sustained bark, as the dogs are trained to alert to live finds using the bark alert required by FEMA.) The first dog was taken away from the area and a second dog was brought in to confirm the indication. The victim was found 20 feet down,

buried in the sugar directly below the dogs' indications.

Irrigation Canal Search—Water

Situation

A five-year-old boy was last seen riding his bike near an irrigation canal one bright and sunny day in May. Divers had been unable to locate the body, although the water appeared from the surface to be flowing slowly. The boy's bike was found near the canal.

Response Teams

Three wilderness search certified dog teams cross-trained in water search were called to assist in the search after five days. In addition to the search dogs, divers were on hand to follow up on any information from the dogs.

Search Area

The search area was defined as the irrigation canal and the surrounding fields. There appeared to be a lot of turbulence below the surface of the water and the channel was full. The water was a cold 38°F from spring mountain runoff. There were bridges spanning the canal and a gate and control wheel that controlled the flow of the water.

Search Description

The dog teams were given their assignment and began to search into the wind blowing from the opposite side of the canal. They followed the flow of the water in the canal. As the dogs worked, one, a black Labrador Retriever, began to alert on scent west of a bridge toward a bend in the canal. The scent appeared to be pooling or collecting at the bend. The same dog again became interested in scent in the water 200 yards downstream from the initial alert at the gate of the control wheel. As the dog team continued to walk along the canal the wind shifted and blew from the opposite direction. The dog turned around to alert to the gate.

Three days later, the divers called the dogs back to the canal to continue to search, since they had not been able to locate the body based on the original alerts from the dogs. The water in the canal was becoming deeper from runoff and visibility was poor due to the murkiness of the water. The area between the bridge and the control wheel gate proved to be an area of continued interest for the same dog that searched it earlier, although it was not as strong as the alert on the previous search.

Outcome

As the team continued to work, the dog became very agitated at a bend in the canal where a drainage pipe intersected the canal. The dog ran to the sandbar between the spillway and the bend in the canal, moving in a grid pattern back and forth as it did when following an air scent during a land search. The dog continued to work toward the spillway and alerted in the vicinity of the spillway out into the

water toward the bend in the canal. The divers recovered the boy's body an hour later from the inside perimeter of the bend in the canal. Although the spillway had been a large scent catch zone, the dog's interest was farther into the canal toward the bend. Apparently, the scent had moved around with the flow of the water throughout the search.

Missing Boy Scout—Wilderness

Situation

A ten-year-old Boy Scout walked away from his camp one night, leaving his scout troop and belongings to take a quick break. He failed to return and the scout troop had been searching for the boy throughout the night, through heavy rains. The local search and rescue team was also coordinating a mission to find an elderly woman in another part of the vast wilderness, so their resources were stretched thin.

Response Teams

Several wilderness search dog teams were called in to assist. The air scent teams were divided between the two searches and the only trailing dog was deployed on the search for the young boy.

Search Area

The area to be searched was in a vast wilderness with mountainous terrain. Much of the area was several miles into the wilderness, requiring rigorous hiking. Following a rainy night, the morning was clear and sunny, and it was determined that the trailing dog team would first be flown to the P.L.S. using a helicopter, to establish a direction of travel before sending in air scent dog teams.

Search Description

Immediately upon arriving at the campsite, Isis, a Belgian Malinois certified in trailing, and working off-lead, was presented with the scent article and given the search command. She walked over to the boy's sleeping bag, circled the campsite, and walked deliberately downhill into the woods. The scout leader confirmed that the boy had walked in that direction to relieve himself and never came back.

Following ground scent, Isis continued to work around a stream where scent appeared to have collected. Based on the fact that the dog became very focused on what appeared to be concentrations of scent, the handler believed the boy spent the night in area by the stream.

Continuing on, the dog trailed scent along the base of a cliff face, where she suddenly lifted her nose and ran toward scent blowing from the east as if working an air scent grid pattern. Isis returned to trailing along the cliff face for a short distance when the wind shifted, then followed the scent on the ground toward the east, moving at a faster pace. The handler asked her support person to radio to mission base that it appeared the boy was moving just

ahead of them and staying out of reach.

The weather suddenly changed and it started to rain, with thunder, lightning, and hail. In spite of the conditions, Isis was frantic to continue the search and was becoming more determined with each step. However, for their own safety, the dog team moved under thick trees where the handler and her support person pulled a storm tarp over the team to wait until the lightning stopped.

As soon as the storm passed and the dog started working again, it became clear that Isis was very near the missing boy. In spite of the apparently close proximity to the boy, there was no response to the searchers' calls and whistles. Isis began to run forward while trailing, then back to the handler. At that point, the handler radioed to mission base and described what the dog was doing. She emphasized that she believed the boy was running away from the team.

Outcome

The mission leader sent a foot team into the area from the opposite direction of the dog team in an attempt to contain the area and the boy. The strategy worked and the boy was found.

The trailing dog found the Boy Scout within a few hours of searching, and he admitted that he had been trying to get away. He heard the dog and the searchers, but had determined not to answer until he heard the scout leader's voice. He also revealed that he had, in fact, spent the night at the stream identified by Isis earlier in the search. The total time for searching was four hours including the helicopter ride into the search area, although additional time was spent catching up with the victim.

City Flood—Disaster

Situation

A sudden flood in Fort Collins, Colorado, buried parts of the town, Colorado State University, and a trailer park in water and thick, oozing mud. Originally, 23 people were missing.

Response Teams

Several local search dog teams were called in to assist in the search and rescue efforts. The dog teams were comprised of wilderness and disaster certified teams.

Search Area

The flood directly affected much of the city and the university. The search area included open spaces, roads, the interior and exterior of buildings, a jumble of trailers, and partially buried cars.

Search Description

On the first day, as Ann, a FEMA Type I canine search specialist approached the search area she noticed a relatively small pool of water with some slight circulation. A Styrofoam cup was slowly circling on the top of the water, so it appeared on the surface as though there was some slow drainage that was blocked. The incident commander asked for a drain map to determine the structure of the underground drains and see where the water was backing up.

On the second day, Ann noticed that the small pool of water had been dug out and a culvert was exposed. Jenner, her search dog, jumped on top of the culvert in the pond to look into it and slid on the slippery mud covering the culvert's surface. Suddenly, Jenner fell into what was remaining of the water and paddled across to get to the front of the culvert, into which he was immediately pulled by the suction without warning. Ann's colleague, Matt, leaped onto the culvert and grabbed the dog's shoulders, then his ears, as the black Labrador Retriever was sucked deeper into the culvert and disappeared.

Ann ran to a manhole several yards away and hung upside down in the drain in an attempt to see the dog. She saw a network of drains with many turns, bends, and slants in the pipe, but no dog. Incident Command still had no maps of the drains, but remembered an opening 1,500 feet away from the culvert. Ann looked into the opening and was able to see the dog buried in the sludge with only six to eight inches of air space. The dog was being carried slowly toward the opening by the sludge, with only his nostrils and eyes visible. All the searchers grabbed his body, pulled him out, and carried him to a vehicle so he could be transported to Colorado State University's veterinary medicine school, only a few blocks away. Jenner refused to lower his head or relax his neck, but he did lick Matt's face, the searcher who tried to save him. Jenner received emergency care for extreme, almost irreversible shock and severe bruising to his chest.

Outcome

This accident was the catalyst for a review and revision of search and rescue protocols concerning safety following a disaster. Jenner survived to continue his search career, but a child may not have been as lucky.

Buried Skiers— Avalanche

Situation

In the winter of 1987 a large and devastating avalanche, in which nine skiers were involved, occurred in Breckenridge, Colorado, out of the bounds of the ski resort. Peak 7 is a large bowl area and was identified as being prone to avalanche by warning signs. Two skiers decided to hike to the top of the bowl to ski down, because no easy access was available. They passed three signs designating the area as dangerous and off limits to skiers, and there were other people already skiing lower down in

the bowl. People riding a chair lift up to Peak 8 suddenly saw two avalanches run concurrently down Peak 7 into the bowl. Four skiers were completely buried, two were buried partially, and three were caught by the slide but not buried.

Response Teams

Ski patrollers from the resort began to search with beacons almost immediately, and 83 people responded to assist in the first hour of the tragedy. Patti Burnett, an avalanche dog handler on the scene, describes the resources used on this search in her book, *Avalanche! Hasty Search, The Training and Care of the Avalanche Rescue Dog.* "Some of the equipment used for this mission included a helicopter, four snowcats, 16 snowmobiles, two metal detectors, a ground radar unit, a command trailer, two ambulances, 130 probe poles, two tents, two generators, and 60 radios." Burnett and her newly certified avalanche dog, Hasty, were dispatched, along with three other avalanche dogs, on the first day.

Search Area

The slide was a combination of hard and soft snow slabs. The length of the slide was 1,600 vertical feet with the fracture of the combined slides measuring 1,300 feet wide and up to 10 feet deep. The resulting debris depth was up to 18 feet. Once settled, the debris filled a third of the bottom of the slide path. Because of the immediate response from emergency agencies, the search area was covered with searchers, backpacks and other gear, probe lines, and a warming area.

Search Description

"By 5:00 P.M. there were 200 rescuers on the deposition. At 5:15 P.M., a probe line located one of the victims beneath four feet of snow," Burnett writes. On the second day the rescue dogs worked the deposition zone throughout the day, in spite of the severe contamination from volunteer searchers, their food, and other distractions. Metal detectors and searchers with probe poles found the second and third victims, four and seven feet below the snow.

On the third day of the search, Burnett and the avalanche dog handlers from Utah realized that generators, which had been set up for the warming tents and the coroner, were saturating the deposition with fumes, "making it impossible for the dogs to find scent," according to Burnett. The tents were relocated on the last day, and Hasty was able to alert on the last body from the top of the deposition. The victim was buried 30 feet from the top of the deposition zone.

Outcome

This avalanche initiated an aggressive avalanche education program for the public and influenced representatives from the U.S. Forest Service, sheriffs and county offices to begin to discuss and change ski area boundary management, which had been an issue for some time.

The management of avalanche search procedures was also redesigned and the result is well-thought-out and defined avalanche response guidelines throughout the mountain states.

Mountain Reservoir Search— Water

Situation

A search at a large mountain reservoir presented searchers with some of the dilemmas that many water search dogs handlers face. A fishing boat capsized with four people on board on Bureau of Land Management (B.L.M.) land during a bad thunderstorm. The missing man had helped the other people get to shore and drowned while trying to swim through the waves.

Response Teams

Two dogs were called in to assist a full month after the drowning when the body failed to surface.

Search Area

The water temperature was 50 degrees and the winds were two to four miles per hour. The depth of the water was 20 to 50 feet. The reservoir covers several hundred acres. When it was created, ranches, canyons, a railroad track, and an existing creek were flooded. There was also the dam spillway and several coves around the reservoir.

Search Description

Divers had been searching the cove where the boat went down during the previous month, but were unable to locate the body. There was heavy silting in the bottom of the reservoir, which dropped the visibility for the divers down to less than a foot when it was disturbed. Some images were visible with sonar, but proved to be equipment from the boat, not the body of the victim. When the dogs arrived they were taken to the cove where the accident occurred, although the divers felt certain the body would not be found there.

One dog, Mariah, a Labrador Retriever, was deployed to search the shoreline of the cove where the boat sank, while the other dog searched the water in the cove from a boat. Winds were out of the south, so the dog team on the shore searched on the cove's north shore, making six passes. Mariah, a wilderness air scent and water-certified search dog, alerted three times toward the opening of the cove into the reservoir during her search passes. Jayne, her handler, drew a line on the map in the direction of each alert from the location of the dog, based on the wind direction. The dog in the boat also alerted in the cove and a marker was placed at that point. The dog handlers felt confident the body was in the cove, although they were unable to pinpoint its location with only one pass of the whole area.

The dog teams switched places as the winds shifted and the search dog with the B.L.M., a German Shepherd Dog named Gretta, searched along the shore of the cove opposite the shore that was originally searched. Mariah and her handler went into the cove in the boat. They searched in a grid pattern from west to east in the cove with the winds from the north. Mariah alerted to a specific area where a buoy was dropped from Gretta's initial alert. The dog showed no additional interest as the boat approached the mouth of the cove.

One of the questions the dog handlers asked themselves was how much silt could have moved in the month since the accident. Also, could the dogs be alerting on the clothing and equipment thrown from the boat? The dogs' alerts were lined up and the area where the scent appeared to be emanating was circled on the map.

Outcome

The divers were unable to locate the body in the specific area immediately, although the search area had been effectively limited. Two weeks after the dog teams first identified the area where the victim's scent rose to the surface of the water, the body was located, floating 37 feet below the surface of the water and suspended in a thermocline. The alerts from the dogs were lined up directly with the location of the body and no more than ten feet to the side. The divers believe they had been swimming above and below the body while searching, but the poor visibility made it impossible to see the body. It was also determined that the body had been covered by silt in the early stages of the search, so was not easily visible either to sonar or to the divers. The trained water search dogs pinpointed the body's location within two hours of searching.

Missing Toddler— Wilderness

Situation

A three-year-old boy and his sister were hiking with a group of adults on an outing in Rocky Mountain National Park on a bright October day. The boy and his sister were enjoying the freedom and the warmth of the day as they played hide-and-seek with each other along the trail. Suddenly, the boy disappeared and couldn't be found by his sister. As the adult hikers rounded a curve in the trail they realized he wasn't there.

Response Teams

All available resources were called to begin the search for the missing child immediately. Dogs were sent in every direction and a trailing dog was deployed from the P.L.S. The trailing dog worked for four miles, but was unable to locate any clues. The air scent dogs were all deployed throughout various search areas. Helicopters, civil air patrol planes, and ground searchers were brought in to search the area as well, focus-ing on areas where a little boy could reasonably hike. A dog trained to track lions for the Division of Wildlife was also brought in to search when tracks from three mountain lions were spotted in the area. Cadaver dogs were also deployed after a few days had passed.

Search Area

The areas searched included streams and rivers. The mountain-sides were generally steep and cov-ered with pine trees, aspens, scrub oak, and boulders. There were also steep, narrow canyons that cut through the region. Terrain that was too dangerous to cover on foot was searched by air.

Search Description

The search continued for two weeks with no clues found. Many trained searchers and volunteers worked long hours in an attempt to find the child. While searching, one of the helicopters crash-landed in a steep canyon, severely injuring per-sonnel who were evacuated from some of the worst terrain in the search area, further risking the safety of the searchers. Search dog teams and ground searchers continued to search the area on their own time for the next few years in fruitless attempts to answer the question, "What happened?"

Outcome

Three years later, during a warm day in the summer, hikers noticed some cloth among fallen branches and pine needles, well off the trail in one of the steepest canyons. The little boy's father identified them as the clothes and a shoe worn by his son on the day he disappeared. The clothes were shredded in places and his shoes showed signs of animal bite marks. They had clearly been ripped and chewed by at least one animal. Another search began in the steep canyon that was too difficult for a little boy to have hiked through. Searchers found the child's skull and a baby tooth buried under a log. It was determined that he'd been probably been killed by a mountain lion; most likely one whose tracks were identified by searchers during the original search. The lion had apparently grabbed the child while he was playing hide-and-seek and immediately carried him off, up the steep canyon, before anyone knew what happened.

It's believed the child was killed instantly, based on the behavior of mountain lions when attacking their prey. However, many questions arose from this search. The wilderness search dogs, experienced in scent discrimination, were given scent articles on the mission, so they were expected to be able to locate his scent. The search dogs were also very experienced in locating young children, but what were the critical features of this search that made it different? What affect does the fresh scent of a predatory animal have on the scent of a missing person, if any? Can a trailing dog trail ground scent when an animal is carrying the victim? The canyon was steep and narrow, so it appears as if none of the air scent dogs were ever in a position to find the boy's scent from their search positions, but is that true?

This search raises many questions for all search and rescue personnel and will continue to haunt the search dog handlers who worked hard to bring resolution to the child's family. Dog handlers will continue to hone their skills and those of their dogs to increase the probability of success on every mission.

Chapter Fifteen

Conclusion

Technology has yet to match the remarkable contributions that trained dogs make to search and rescue. Whether air scenting or trailing, search dogs willingly offer their skills and capabilities to meet the broad range of needs in the world today. People are only beginning to understand the incredible resource dogs provide to humankind. In spite of the developments in technology, many people return to dogs as their most reliable and trusted partners.

Search dogs and their handlers base their work together on the bond and love they share as they grow to become the best resource available in search and rescue. The dog team is a true example of the whole being greater than its individual parts. Without the trust and understanding that develop from long, sometimes arduous hours of working together, search dog teams would be very limited in their results.

Search dogs and their handlers contribute more than time and energy to provide their service. They share a passion for adventure and exciting challenges, as well as a respect for the dangers they face on each mission. Most importantly, they share the love of working together in close and satisfying partnerships, the memory of which lasts a lifetime.

The author (right) and her search dog Chi Tri Sorts Isis des Anges find a happy "victim."

Glossary

Air scenting—The dog's ability to identify scent in the air as it's emanating directly from a person.

Alert—Trained behavior used to indicate a search dog's find when air scenting. The way the dog alerts the handler to its find varies and is based on the handler's preference for that particular specialty.

Avalanche rescue—Searching for people buried when snow collapses and slides down a mountainside.

Bark alert—A type of alert used, especially by disaster response dogs and often by avalanche dogs, in which the dog barks continuously to indicate that it has found the source of scent.

Cadaver search—Search involving scent source from human tissue, blood, other body fluids, and materials that have been handled and worn by humans.

Cross-training—Training dogs for more than a single discipline.

Deposition zone—In an avalanche, the deposition zone is the area where the snow runs out or settles; it is also known as the debris field.

Directed send—Hand signals used by handlers to send their search dog into a specific area of a search. The directed send is required for disaster response dogs and avalanche dogs.

Disaster Search and Rescue—Searching for people buried in mudslides or collapsed structures following a disaster. FEMA disaster response dogs are certified to locate live victims. Some disaster response dogs search for cadaver material.

Drive—An instinctive impulse that urges a dog to some action. The type and intensity of drives varies from dog to dog.

FEMA—Federal Emergency Management Agency, was founded as an independent federal agency in 1979 to reduce loss from all types of catastophic dangers through a program of emergency management.

Fight or flight—A defense drive, defined as a dog's intention to protect itself and/or its territory from invaders.

Hot load—Boarding a helicopter while the engine is engaged and the blades are turning. Hot loads

A diver plays with a puppy in the water before hiding.

are common for avalanche rescues, where time is critical.

Human remains detection (H.R.D.)—Human cadaver search and recovery. H.R.D. includes recently deceased bodies as well as decaying bodies, body parts, tissue, and body fluids.

Hunt drive—A dog's willingness or desire to search out, follow, and find the scent of the prey.

Interest—Interest is shown by a search dog in a particular scent or a source of scent. Although interest alone is not trained behavior, an observant handler may make note of the interest in a search if it becomes necessary to return to an area.

Negative indication—When the search dog determines where the victim is not located or did not travel.

Negative trail—A training exercise for trailing dogs in which the handler presents the dog with a scent article that does not belong to the subject the dog is asked to find.

Scent cone—The indefinite pattern formed by scent as it's carried away from the body by the air and breezes.

Scent pool—Areas where scent has collected and is contained.

Search area—A predefined geographic area assigned to an air scent dog team.

Play drive—A dog's desire to engage in entertaining behavior with others or itself.

Point last seen (P.L.S.)—The location where the missing person was last seen.

Prey drive—A dog's eagerness to chase or pursue a fleeing target, such as a toy, an animal, or a person.

Reading the dog—The ability to watch how the dog works and translate that observation into an understanding of the dog's experience.

Recall/refind—A secondary alert when the dog returns to the handler after finding the victim to take the handler to the victim (the refind).

Scent article—An article worn or handled by the missing person upon whom the search is focused, used to identify the individual's scent.

Search and rescue (SAR)—An aspect of emergency services in which federal, state, and local agencies coordinate, deploy, and manage trained, certified teams to look for, rescue, or recover lost and/or injured people.

Secondary indication—When a search dog follows an initial alert to the scent source, with another alert to the handler to show the handler where the victim is found.

Temperature gradient—The difference between the ground temperature and the temperature of the snow covering the ground.

Thermoclines—Temperature differences at different levels in bodies of water.

Tracking—Following the crushed earth and disturbed vegetation from footprints created along an individual's path as he or she walks.

Trailing—Searching for residual scent that settles on the ground as a person walks through an area.

Trained indication—The way the search dog is trained to notify its handler that it has located the source of the scent or the strongest scent in the area. Examples are recall/refind, show me, digging, lie down, and sit.

It is sometimes necessary to keep avalanche dogs warm during breaks.

Urban search and rescue—A FEMA disaster search and rescue discipline used in situations when natural or man-made disasters affect an area.

Water search—Searching for victims of drowning in lakes, streams, or rivers.

Wilderness search and rescue—Searching for missing or lost people in the wilderness. The two scenting techniques used in wilderness search are trailing and air scenting. Sometimes referred to as *area search* when applied to air scent dogs.

Useful Literature and Web Sites

Books

Avalanche! Hasty Search, The Training and Care of the Avalanche Rescue Dog, by Patti Burnett, Doral Publishing, 2003.

Cadaver Dog Handbook: Forensic Training and Tactics for the Recovery of Human Remains, by Andrew J. Rebmann, Marcia Koenig, Edward David, Marcella H. Sorg, CRC Press, 2000.

Dog Heroes, Saving Lives and Protecting America, by Jen Bidner, The Lyons Press, 2002.

Ready! The Training of the Search and Rescue Dog, by Susan Bulanda, Doral Publishing, 1995.

Scent and the Scenting Dog, by William Syrotuck, Barkleigh Publications, 1972.

Scent: Training to Track, Search and Rescue, by Milo D. Pearsall, Hugo Verbruggen, M.D., Alpine Publications, 1982.

Search and Rescue Dogs, Training the K-9 Hero, Second Edition, by American Rescue Dog Association, Howell Book House, 2002.

Wilderness Search and Rescue, by Tim J. Setnicka, Appalachian Mountain Club Books, 1981.

This search dog has learned to trust her handler.

A search dog alerts to the area where scent has risen to the surface of a lake.

Web Sites

National Association of Search and Rescue
www.NASAR.org

Federal Emergency Management Agency
www.FEMA.org

Search and Rescue Internet Directory
www.SARONE.org

FEMA Canine Working Group
www.DisasterDog.org

Institute for Canine Forensics
www.k9forensic.org

Volhard Motivational Method dog training
www.volhard.com

Index

A search dog is rewarded with play.

Some dogs bite at the water to catch the scent.